THE PINEAPPLE COOKBOOK

Patti Donnelly

Bess Press
P. O. Box 22388
Honolulu, Hawaii 96823

TX
811
.D68
1991

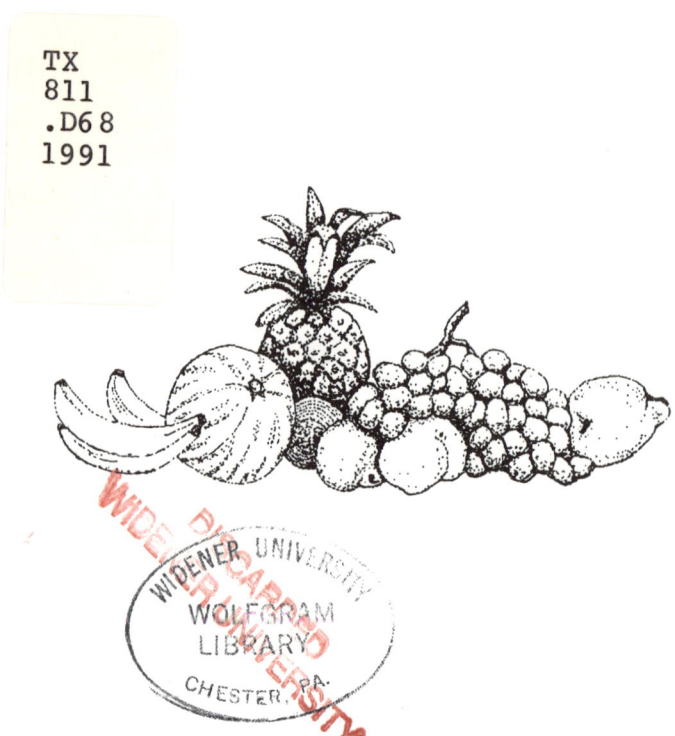

Cover design: Paula Newcomb

Cover art: Patti Donnelly

Illustrations: Patti Donnelly

Editing and typesetting: Revé Shapard

Library of Congress Catalog No.: 91-70848

Donnelly, Patti
  The Pineapple Cookbook
Honolulu, Hawaii: Bess Press, Inc.
128 pages

ISBN: 0-935848-89-4
Copyright © 1991 by The Bess Press, Inc.
ALL RIGHTS RESERVED
Printed in the United States of America

TABLE OF CONTENTS

About This Book   1
About Pineapples   2
Cooking with Pineapples   3

BEVERAGES   7

Holiday Punch   9
Pineapple-Papaya Slush   9
Pineapple-Lime Slush   9
Tropical Fruit Smoothie   10
Pineapple and Strawberry Smoothie   10
Pineapple Cider   11
Lahaina Fizz   11
C.O.P. Cooler   12
Frenchman's Cove Mint Julep   12
Poi Dog   13
Greek Fruit Punch   13
Spiked Pineapple Cinnamon Tea   14

APPETIZERS   15

Pineapple Kebabs   17
Prosciutto and Pineapple Spears   17
Grilled Fruit Kebabs   18
Party Pineapple   18
Champagne Pineapple   19
Broiled Pineapple   19
Salmon Spread   19
Hawaiian Cheese Dip   20
Pineapple-Glazed Brie   20

iii

SALADS   21

Fruit Salads   23
  South Seas Fruit Salad   23
  Pineapple, Strawberry, and Romaine Salad   23
  Laurie's Orange-Pineapple Salad   24
  Islander Salad   24
  Hawaiian Fruit Salad   25
  Fruit and Coconut Salad   25
  Pineapple and Kiwifruit Salad   26
  Pineapple and Avocados   26

Vegetable Salads   27
  Beet and Pineapple Salad   27
  Chinese Broccoli and Pineapple Salad   27
  Curried Pineapple and Sweet Potatoes   28
  Melodi's Curried Carrot Salad   28
  Gingered Sweet Potatoes and Pineapple   29
  Pineapple and Cucumber Salad   30
  Tropical Coleslaw   30
  Mexican Salad   31
  Warm Cheese Salad   32

Rice and Bean Salads   33
  Nutty Pineapple Rice Salad   33
  Lentil and Pineapple Salad with Cilantro   32
  Lentils with Pineapple and Mint   34

Poultry and Seafood Salads   35
  Curried Turkey, Pineapple, and Avocado Salad   35
  Pineapple and Chicken Salad   35
  Curried Chicken Salad with Pineapple   36
  Pineapple Crab Louie   37
  Martha Ann's Pineapple-Lobster Salad   37
  Albacore Salad   38
  Ahi Stuffed Tomatoes   38

BRUNCH AND LUNCH   39

Breakfast Yogurt Hawaiian   41
Broiled Pineapple with Yogurt   41
Breakfast Tamales   42
Pancakes with Fruit Sauce   43
Pineapple French Toast   43
Oatmeal with Honeyed Pineapple   44

Sandwiches   45
  Grilled Breakfast Sandwich   45
  Albacore Salad Sandwich   46
  Ricotta and Pineapple Sandwich   46
  Ham and Cheese Croissant   47
  Canadian Bacon and Pineapple Sandwich   47
  Roast Beef Sandwich   48
  Cheese Quesadillas   48

VEGETABLES AND SIDE DISHES   49

Beets with Pineapple   51
Gingered Pineapple Broccoli   51
Almond Carrots with Pineapple   52
Annie's Green Beans with Pineapple   52
Sweet Potato Soufflé   53
Nicole's Rings of Saturn   53
Martha Ann's Pineapple and Sweet Potatoes   54
Melodi's Sweet Potatoes   55
Pineapple Glazed Yams   56
Marinated Peppers   56
Pineapple and Apricot Compote   57
Curried Rice   57
Brown Rice and Wild Rice   58
South Seas Baked Beans   58
Baked Beans with Fruit   59
Noodles Polynesian   59
Cheesy Pineapple Casserole   60

SEAFOOD, POULTRY, AND MEAT   61

Seafood   63
  Shrimp Teriyaki   63
  Shrimp Tempura   63
  Grilled Shrimp with Pineapple Relish   64
  Baked Scallops with Pineapple   64
  Grilled Scallop Kebabs   65
  Broiled Ahi Steaks with Fresh Pineapple Relish   66
  Marinated Swordfish Kebabs   67

Poultry   67
  South Seas Barbequed Chicken   67
  Stuffed Chicken Breasts   68
  Quick Chicken Roll-Ups   69
  Chicken with Pineapple and Snow Peas   70
  Pineapple Chicken   71
  Chicken and Rice Pineapple Boats   72
  Michel's Luau Chicken   73
  Chicken and Pineapple Pasta   73
  South American Chicken   74
  Glazed Cornish Game Hens   74
  Turkey with Macadamia Nuts and Pineapple   75

Meats   76
  Pete's Pineapple Steak   76
  Flank Steak with Pineapple Relish   77
  Pineapple Stir-Fry   78
  Maui Meatloaf   79
  Pineapple Meatballs   80
  Glazed Roast Loin of Pork   81
  Roast Pork with Onions and Pineapple   81
  Puff Pastry Shells with Ham   82
  Ham Steak Hawaiian   83
  Glazed Ham   84

MUFFINS AND BREADS   85

Martha Ann's Pineapple Muffins   87
Broiled Pineapple Toast   87
Nutty Pineapple Muffins   88
Pineapple Upside-Down Muffins   89
Oat Bran Muffins   90
Pineapple Oat Bran Bread   91
Pineapple Crescents   92

DESSERTS   93

Pies and Pastries   95
   Honolua Pie   95
   Pineapple and Apricot Pie   96
   Melodi's Coconut Pineapple Pie   97
   Pineapple Tart   97
   Cinnamon Pineapple Turnovers   98

Cakes and Cookies   99
   Pineapple Cheesecake   99
   Pineapple Pecan Upside-Down Cake   100
   Eleanor's Upside-Down Cake   101
   Walnut Carrot Cake with Pineapple   102
   Pineapple-Glazed Sponge Cake   103
   Cinnamon Pineapple Cookies   104

Fruit Desserts   104
   Pineapple with Bourbon Cream   104
   Pineapple and Bananas with Cream   105
   Gingered Cream over Pineappple   105
   Molded Pineapple Cream Cheese   106
   Brandied Pineapple   106
   Glazed Pineapple   107
   Fresh Pineapple in Pineapple Wine   107
   Pineapple Flambé   108

Fruit Fondue   108
Baked Rhubarb and Pineapple   109
Bread Pudding   109
Pineapple Custard Crisps   110
Rice Pudding   111
Pineapple Tapioca Pudding   111

Frozen Desserts   112
   Pineapple Sorbet   112
   Pineapple-Lime Sorbet   112

CHUTNEY, JAM, PRESERVES, RELISH, AND SALSA   113

Pineapple Chutney   115
Coconut Pineapple Chutney   115
Spiced Pineapple Chutney   116
Easy Pineapple Jam   116
Pineapple Preserves   117
Melodi's Pineapple Relish   117
Pineapple Salsa   117
Pineapple and Papaya Salsa   118
Pineapple Sauce for Roast Beef   118
Pineapple Sauce for Ham   118

ABOUT THIS BOOK

When I first moved to Maui a friend brought me a pineapple fresh from the fields, still covered in red dirt. After one bite, with the juice still dripping off my chin, I knew I was hooked. I had fallen in love with this lush, juicy tropical fruit.

As time went on, my friend kept bringing me pineapples and I kept preparing them the only way I knew how–chilled and sliced. I had vague childhood memories of those cakes with sweet pineapple rings on top that were forever turning up at potlucks, family reunions, and PTA events. And, of course, those little cans of fruit cocktail that included pineapple tidbits.

But, there had to be more that could be done with such an elegant fruit. In search of new ways to prepare my favorite fruit, I started asking friends and family, "How do you like to eat pineapple?" As the recipes started coming in, I was amazed by the variety of ways people prepared pineapple. The quest went further. I started asking friends of friends, people at the beauty shop, on airplanes, in doctor's offices, in shopping centers, fellow aspiring artists in my art classes, and even strangers on the street, "How do you like to eat pineapple?" Before long, I had quite a collection of diverse recipes, well over a hundred, ranging from gourmet to holistic natural food to fast food. So that's what this book is, a collection of pineapple recipes. It is as diverse as the people who were willing to share their recipes with me.

I especially want to acknowledge and thank the following, for not only their recipes but their encouragement, support, and love: Bea Gordon, Melodi Lockhart, Martha Ann Rice, Hazel Shumway, Dr. S. Michel Skolnick, the man on the plane, the woman at Kaahumanu Center with the charming daughter, and all those generous people who shared their recipes without my getting their names. And George, thanks for the pineapples.

ABOUT PINEAPPLES

The pineapple has a long, varied, and interesting history. Originally from Brazil, it was already being enjoyed throughout South and Central America by the time Christopher Columbus arrived in 1493. It was on the island of Guadaloupe, in the Caribbean, where Columbus exchanged a few trinkets for his first pineapple.

The local islanders, who cultivated it, not only looked upon the pineapple as a delicious fruit, but had also discovered many other uses for it. They drank its juice as a digestive aid. The women used pineapple as a beauty aid to improve the texture of their skin, and the warriors used the flesh to help heal their wounds.

Columbus took the pineapple back to Europe, where it became the symbol of hospitality and a luxury available only to the aristocracy. It became so popular in England that a certain nobleman graciously rented pineapples for festive occasions. In France, it became known as the "King of Fruit," due to King Louis XIV's passion for pineapple.

The islanders who gave Christopher Columbus his first pineapple weren't the only ones to find pineapple to be more than just a delicious tropical fruit. Today, biochemists are investigating a wide range of applications. Bromelain, the protein digestive agent of the pineapple plant, has been used successfully in the treatment of a wide variety of diseases. Medical literature during the past twenty-five years describes bromelain's role in the treatment of arthritis, digestive disorders, migraine headaches, and even heart disease.

Nobody seems to know when pineapples first arrived in Hawaii. The earliest written account was a diary entry recorded in 1813 by Don Francisco de Paula y Marin, a Spanish horticulturist. He casually mentions planting pineapples and an orange tree.

The Hawaiians looked upon the pineapple as an outsider. They named it Halakahiki, meaning a screw-pine from a foreign land.

Pineapples may have been a newcomer to Hawaii, but it didn't remain a foreigner very long. By the mid-1800s pineapples were being successfully cultivated as well as growing wild. It wasn't until 1901 that a commercial plantation or cannery was operating. That was the year James Dole organized on Oahu the first of today's modern pineapple companies. On Maui the Baldwin family began pineapple operations in 1903 and continue today as the Maui Pineapple Company.

The pineapple is now a symbol of Hawaii. Most of us, when we think of pineapple, think of Hawaiian pineapple.

COOKING WITH PINEAPPLES

When you purchase your fresh pineappple, choose the ripest one you can find. After they're picked, pineapples no longer increase in sweetness, but only get softer. Determining ripeness is the tricky part, since neither the appearance of the skin nor the color denotes ripeness. Perhaps the most reliable indications are a dull, solid sound when the finger is snapped against the side of the fruit, and a full, fruity fragrance. Also, look for a pineapple that is heavy with juice and has a fresh, lively plume. Some people say they look for a soft spot on the bottom. Others like to be able to remove one of the leaves with a neat little tug.

Pineapples are in season year round, but the ones available during the summer tend to be a little sweeter because of the longer days with more abundant sunshine.

The majority of pineapples found fresh in the grocery store range in size from 3 to 4 pounds. The larger ones tend to be a better buy; after all; there's more edible flesh to enjoy.

Fresh pineapples store best at about 50 degrees, away from direct sunlight. But they do quite well at room temperature.

Once you have selected your fresh pineapple, it's time to cut it. Everyone I talked to seems to have a favorite way to cut a pineapple. Here are five of the more popular ways. Choose one that fits the recipe you're going to use and have fun.

1- Grasp the crown firmly. (Caution: the leaves have sharp points!) Cut off the rind with a sharp knife. Remove the eyes by paring the pineapple diagonally. Slice off the crown and the bottom of the fruit. The pineapple can now be cut into slices or wedges. Remove the core if desired.

2-Cut off the crown and the bottom of the pineapple. Then slice the pineapple crosswise. Peel the slices and remove the core.

3-Slice off the top of the pineapple. Cut down and around the inside of the fruit, removing the flesh in chunks. The resulting pineapple shell can be used, frozen, and reused to serve pineapple salads, fruit combinations, or ice creams and sorbets.

4-Cut the pineapple lengthwise, top to bottom through the center, leaves and all. This results in two halves that are perfect for hollowing out and refilling for a spectacular way to serve a pineapple dish.

5-For those of us who are not particularly accomplished with knives, there is a special cutter that resembles a wheel. After cutting off the top of the pineapple with a knife, use this cutter to simultaneously core, peel, and cut the pineapple into fingers.

Pineapple is also available canned, and it is one of the more successful canned fruits.

Pineapple is packed in either unsweetened pineapple juice or syrup. It is available in either 8-ounce or 20-ounce sizes in your grocery store. The 8-ounce container yields 1 cup of pineapple, while the 20-ounce container yields 2-1/2 cups. The canned pineapple is available in several different styles, including slices, chunks, crushed, and tidbits.

In recipes containing any gelatin mixture, remember to use canned pineapple or fresh pineapple that has been cooked first.

Recipes

Beverages

BEVERAGES

Holiday Punch
Pineapple-Papaya Slush
Pineapple-Lime Slush
Tropical Fruit Smoothie
Pineapple and Strawberry Smoothie
Pineapple Cider
Lahaina Fizz
C.O.P. Cooler
Frenchman's Cove Mint Julep
Poi Dog
Greek Fruit Punch
Spiked Pineapple Cinnamon Tea

Holiday Punch

4 cups cranberry juice cocktail
2 cups pineapple juice
2 quarts ginger ale

Combine chilled juices in serving container. Add ginger ale and ice cubes just before serving.

Pineapple-Papaya Slush

1 ripe papaya, peeled and seeded
1 cup pineapple juice
1 cup apple juice
2 cups ice

Blend all ingredients in blender until smooth.

Pineapple-Lime Slush

1 cup fresh pineapple chunks
1/2 cucumber, peeled and seeded
2 tablespoons lime juice
2 cups ice

Blend all ingredients in blender until smooth.

Tropical Fruit Smoothie

1 cup apple juice
1/4 fresh papaya
1/2 banana
1/2 cup fresh pineappple chunks

Arrange fruit in single layer on baking sheet lined with wax paper. Freeze. Blend all ingredients in blender until smooth. Serves 1.

Pineapple and Strawberry Smoothie

1 cup milk
1/2 cup pineapple chunks
1/2 cup strawberries

Arrange fruit in single layer on baking sheet lined with wax paper. Freeze. Blend all ingredients in blender until smooth. Serves 1.

Pineapple Cider

1 quart apple cider
1 cup pineapple juice
2 cups orange juice
1/4 cup brown sugar
7 whole cloves
2 sticks cinnamon

Combine all ingredients in a saucepan. Bring to a boil. Reduce heat and simmer 5 minutes. Remove cloves and cinnamon sticks. Serve in mugs. Serves 6 - 8.

Lahaina Fizz

6 ounces light rum
2 cups chilled pineapple juice
Juice from 4 limes
Chilled club soda
4 lime slices for garnish

Mix the rum with the pineapple and lime juices. Pour into 4 tall glasses filled with ice. Top off rum and fruit juices with chilled club soda. Garnish with the lime slices. Serves 4.

C.O.P. (Cherry, Orange and Pineapple) Cooler

3 cups orange juice
1 cup pineapple juice
Juice from 4 lemons
4 ounces Kirschwasser (cherry liqueur)

Fill 4 glasses with ice and pour 1 ounce of Kirschwasser into each. Combine the fruit juices and divide among the glasses. Serves 4.

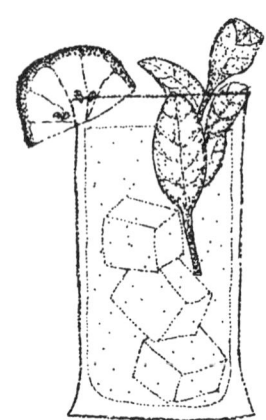

Frenchman's Cove Mint Julep

1 small pineapple, peeled, cored, and cubed
1/2 cup mint leaves
1/2 cup sugar
4 cups crushed ice
1 cup bourbon
Juice from 1 lime
4 dashes angostura bitters
4 long sprigs fresh mint
Powdered sugar

Purée pineapple with mint and sugar, add crushed ice and process until smooth. Stir in bourbon, lime juice, and bitters. Serve in well-chilled glasses. Garnish with mint sprigs that have been dipped in the powdered sugar. Serves 4.

Poi Dog

For each drink:
1 cup pineapple juice
1 ounce vodka
Crushed ice

Fill glass with crushed ice. Add pineapple juice and vodka. Stir.

Greek Fruit Punch
(Sampania Me Frouta Kai Krasi)

2 bananas, sliced
1 fresh pineapple, peeled, cored, and cut into chunks
1 cup brandy
2 oranges, sliced
1 bottle chilled champagne
2 bottles chilled Greek Maurodaphne wine (or use a rosé wine)
2 bottles club soda
Fresh strawberries, sliced
Mint leaves

Marinate bananas and pineapple in the brandy at least 2 hours. Place in punchbowl and add orange slices, champagne, wine, and club soda. Garnish with strawberries and mint leaves.

Spiked Pineapple Cinnamon Tea

2 cinnamon tea bags
2 cups pineapple juice
2 tablespoons sugar
1/4 cup rum

Heat pineapple juice to a boil in saucepan. Remove from heat and add tea bags. Cover and let stand 5 minutes. Remove tea bags, add sugar and rum, stir well and serve warm. Serves 2.

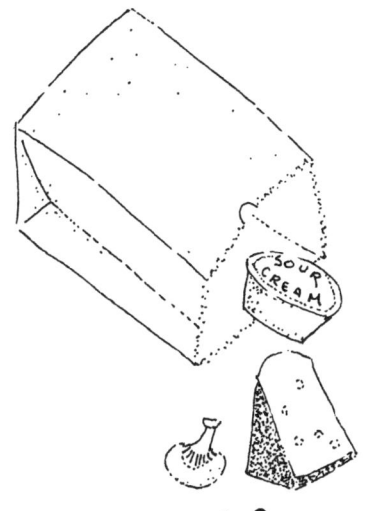

Appetizers

APPETIZERS

Pineapple Kebabs
Prosciutto and Pineapple Spears
Grilled Fruit Kebabs
Party Pineapple
Champagne Pineapple
Broiled Pineapple
Salmon Spread
Hawaiian Cheese Dip
Pineapple-Glazed Brie

Pineapple Kebabs

Using bamboo skewers, alternate fresh pineapple chunks with any of the following combinations:

- Cheddar and ham cubes
- Strawberries marinated in orange liqueur
- Meatballs
- Cooked shrimp
- Barbecued chicken nuggets
- Cubes of grilled lamb and stuffed olives

To serve, cut pineapple lengthwise, from top to bottom, through leaves and all. Put flat side down on serving platter. Spear with the kebabs.

Prosciutto and Pineapple Spears

8 fresh pineapple spears
8 slices prosciutto (or Virginia ham)
Freshly ground pepper

Wrap each pineapple spear with a slice of prosciutto (or Virginia ham). Hold in place with a toothpick. Serve with freshly ground pepper.

Grilled Fruit Kebabs

These are great served with pork or ham steaks.

1 small pineapple, peeled, cored, and cubed
3 bananas, thickly sliced
2 apples, cored and cubed
2 oranges, sectioned
1 cup pineapple juice
3 tablespoons Triple Sec

Marinate fruit in a mixture of the pineapple juice and the Triple Sec for about 15 minutes. Thread fruit on skewers and baste often with the marinade while broiling or grilling. Cook for about 5 minutes, turning often.

Party Pineapple

1 pineapple
1 orange, peeled and sectioned
1 cup seedless grapes
2 peaches, sliced
1 tablespoon sugar
4 tablespoons Grand Marnier

Slice off the top (crown) of the pineapple, remove flesh and cut into cubes, reserving the shell. Toss the cubed pineapple with the other fruits; sprinkle with the sugar and the Grand Marnier. Let fruit rest 2 hours. Return all of the fruit to the shell and pour the juices over the top to moisten. Top the pineapple with its crown, wrap with plastic wrap and chill until serving time.

Champagne Pineapple

Colorful fruit combinations, such as this, served in pineapple shells, can substitute for flowers on the buffet table.

1 pineapple
1 cantaloupe
1/4 watermelon
2 cups champagne

Chill the fruit. Make melon balls out of the watermelon and cantaloupe. Slice the top off the pineapple, remove the flesh and cut into cubes, reserving the shell. Toss the cubed pineapple with melon balls and fill the pineapple shell. Pour the chilled champagne over the fruit and serve.

Broiled Pineapple

8 fresh pineapple spears
8 slices bacon

Fasten bacon around pineapple spears with toothpicks. Broil under moderate heat. Serve warm.

Salmon Spread

1 can salmon, skin and bones removed
1 (20-ounce) can pineapple tidbits, drained
8 ounces cream cheese
10 black olives, chopped
1 small onion, minced
2 tablespoons parsley
Dash cayenne pepper
Celery sticks

Combine finely chopped salmon with remaining ingredients. Serve with celery sticks.

Hawaiian Cheese Dip

1 cup ricotta
1/4 cup brown sugar
8-ounce package cream cheese
2 tablespoons lemon juice
1 (8-ounce) can pineapple tidbits, drained

Blend all of the ingredients together. Chill well. Serve with crackers, vegetables or fruit.

Pineapple-Glazed Brie

3 cups fresh pineapple, diced
3/4 cup brown sugar
1/3 cup water
1/4 teaspoon prepared mustard
1/4 teaspoon minced fresh ginger
1/8 teaspoon allspice
1 Brie cheese wheel (8-inch diameter)
2 tablespoons slivered almonds

Combine all of the ingredients except for the cheese and almonds in a saucepan and cook, stirring frequently, for about 5 minutes. Cool to room temperature. Place the cheese on a baking sheet. Using a sharp knife, carefully remove the top rind from the cheese. Don't cut through the side rind. Spread the pineapple mixture over the Brie. Bake the cheese at 300 degrees for 10-12 minutes, until soft. Cool slightly and serve with crackers.

Salads

SALADS

Fruit Salads
  South Seas Fruit Salad
  Pineapple, Strawberry, and Romaine Salad
  Laurie's Orange-Pineapple Salad
  Islander Salad
  Hawaiian Fruit Salad
  Fruit and Coconut Salad
  Pineapple and Kiwifruit Salad
  Pineapple and Avocados

Vegetable Salads
  Beet and Pineapple Salad
  Chinese Broccoli and Pineapple Salad
  Curried Pineapple and Sweet Potatoes
  Melodi's Curried Carrot Salad
  Gingered Sweet Potatoes and Pineapple
  Pineapple and Cucumber Salad
  Tropical Coleslaw
  Mexican Salad
  Warm Cheese Salad

Rice and Bean Salads
  Nutty Pineapple Rice Salad
  Lentil and Pineapple Salad with Cilantro
  Lentils with Pineapple and Mint

Poultry and Seafood Salads
  Curried Turkey, Pineapple, and Avocado Salad
  Pineapple and Chicken Salad
  Curried Chicken Salad with Pineapple
  Pineapple Crab Louie
  Martha Ann's Pineapple-Lobster Salad
  Albacore Salad
  Ahi Stuffed Tomatoes

South Seas Fruit Salad

1 tablespoon poppy seeds
1 teaspoon dry mustard
1/4 teaspoon cumin
1/3 cup pineapple juice
1/2 cup yogurt
1 tablespoon orange juice
1/2 teaspoon lemon juice
1 cup fresh pineapple cubes
1 papaya, peeled, seeded, and cubed
1 apple, cubed
1 banana, sliced
Bibb lettuce
Sunflower seeds

In a jar combine the poppy seeds, dry mustard, cumin, pineapple juice, yogurt, orange juice, and lemon juice. Cover and shake well. Combine the fruits and then arrange them on lettuce-lined salad plates. Pour dressing over salad, sprinkle with sunflower seeds and serve. Serves 4.

Pineapple, Strawberry, and Romaine Salad

1/4 cup champagne vinegar
2 tablespoons vegetable oil
1/4 teaspoon sugar
1 head romaine, torn into bite-sized pieces
1 cup watercress, trimmed
3/4 cup sliced strawberries
3/4 cup fresh pineapple, diced
2 celery stalks, sliced
1 tablespoon slivered almonds

In a jar combine the vinegar, oil, and sugar. Add salt and pepper to taste. Cover and shake well. Combine remaining ingredients, add dressing and toss well. Serves 4.

Laurie's Orange-Pineapple Salad

2 cups fresh pineapple cubes
2 oranges, peeled and sectioned
Brown sugar

Combine pineapple cubes and orange sections. Sprinkle with brown sugar and serve. Serves 4.

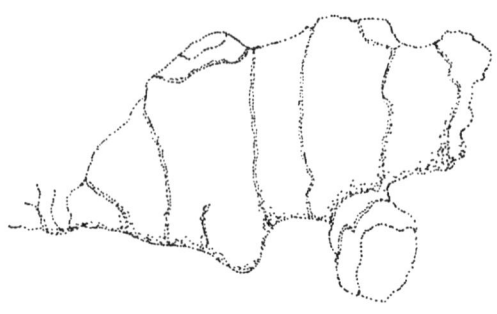

Islander Salad

Lettuce leaves for 4 salads
2 cups fresh pineapple cubes
1/2 cup chopped nuts
1/2 cup pineapple juice
1 tablespoon grated fresh ginger
6 tablespoons vegetable oil
1/2 teaspoon salt
1 tablespoon lemon juice
3 tablespoons vinegar
1 teaspoon sugar

Arrange the lettuce leaves on 4 salad plates. Layer the pineapple over the lettuce leaves. Sprinkle with nuts. Combine the remaining ingredients in a jar and shake to mix well. Drizzle over the salads and serve. Serves 4.

Hawaiian Fruit Salad

1 pint strawberries
1 small pineapple, peeled, cored, and cut into chunks
1 papaya, peeled, seeded, and cubed
2 kiwifruit, peeled and cubed
Boston lettuce leaves
1/4 teaspoon salt
Dash pepper
1/8 teaspoon prepared mustard
2 tablespoons lemon juice
3 tablespoons pineapple juice
6 tablespoons safflower oil

On four individual serving plates arrange the fruit over the lettuce leaves. Make the dressing by combining all of the remaining ingredients in a jar. Cover and shake well. Pour the dressing over the fruit and serve. Serves 4.

Fruit and Coconut Salad

For a buffet, cut the pineapple in half lengthwise, from top to bottom through leaves and all. Remove the flesh and serve the fruit salad in the shell.

1 orange, peeled and sliced
1 papaya, peeled, seeded, and cubed
1 pint strawberries, sliced
1 apple, diced
1 banana, sliced
1 pineapple, peeled, cored, and cubed
3 tablespoons grated coconut

Mix all of the fruit in a large bowl and top with the coconut. Serves 4.

Pineapple and Kiwifruit Salad

1 pineapple, peeled, cored, and cubed
4 kiwifruit, peeled and cut into wedges
Juice from two lemons
2 tablespoons sugar
Bibb lettuce leaves

Combine the fruit, lemon, and sugar in a bowl. Cover and chill one hour. Arrange fruit over lettuce-lined salad plates and serve. Serves 4.

Pineapple and Avocados

2 avocados, peeled and sliced
8 slices fresh pineapple
8 leaves Bibb lettuce
1 tablespoon sugar
1/2 teaspoon mustard
1 teaspoon celery seed
1 tablespoon minced shallot
1/2 cup vegetable oil
3 tablespoons lemon juice
Salt and pepper to taste

Layer avocado and pineapple slices over the lettuce. Whisk together the remaining ingredients. Pour over the salad and serve. Serves 4.

Beet and Pineapple Salad

Vegetable oil
1 pound beets
1 cup fresh pineapple cubes
3 tablespoons lemon juice

Wash beets; then rub with vegetable oil. Bake in 400-degree oven until tender, about 1-1/4 hours. Chill well, peel, and cut into cubes. Combine the pineapple and beets with the lemon juice just before serving. Season to taste with salt and pepper. Serves 4.

Chinese Broccoli and Pineapple Salad

1 bunch broccoli spears
1 clove garlic, minced
1 tablespoon sesame oil
1 tablespoon vegetable oil
1 teaspoon soy sauce
1 tablespoon lime juice
2 tablespoons rice vinegar
1 teaspoon minced fresh ginger
2 cups fresh pineapple cubes

Steam broccoli spears until tender, rinse in cold water and drain. Combine remaining ingredients except for the pineapple in a jar, cover and shake well. Combine the broccoli spears with the pineapple and dressing and serve. Serves 4.

Curried Pineapple and Sweet Potatoes

1 pound sweet potatoes
1/2 cup pineapple tidbits, drained
2 tablespoons raisins
2 tablespoons slivered almonds
1/4 cup pineapple juice
1 tablespoon vegetable oil
1 teaspoon sugar
1/8 teaspoon curry powder
Lettuce leaves

Peel and cube sweet potatoes and boil until just tender. In a bowl combine the sweet potato cubes with the pineapple tidbits, raisins, and almonds. In a saucepan combine the pineapple juice, vegetable oil, sugar, and curry powder. Bring to a boil; then pour over the sweet potato mixture. Toss to coat well, cool slightly and serve over the lettuce leaves. Serves 4.

Melodi's Curried Carrot Salad

1 cup mayonnaise
1-1/2 teaspoons curry powder
1/4 teaspoon salt
1 pound carrots, grated
1/2 cup raisins
1 cup fresh pineapple, small chunks

Combine mayonnaise, curry powder, and salt. Mix together grated carrots, raisins, and the pineapple. Toss with the mayonnaise dressing and serve. Serves 4.

Gingered Sweet Potatoes and Pineapple

1 pound sweet potatoes, cut into 1-inch cubes
2 tablespoons vegetable oil
2 tablespoons butter, melted
1 tablespoon lemon juice
1/2 cup chopped walnuts
1/2 cup pineapple cubes
2 teaspoons minced fresh gingerroot
2 tablespoons vegetable oil
2 tablespoons vinegar
1 minced garlic clove
Lettuce leaves
2 green onions, sliced
1/4 pound crisp bacon pieces

Pat sweet potato pieces dry; then sauté in the vegetable oil until golden. Drain well. Combine melted butter and lemon juice in a baking dish with the sweet potatoes, nuts, pineapple and gingerroot. Salt and pepper to taste. Bake at 400 degrees for about 15 minutes, or until tender. Combine the 2 tablespoons vegetable oil with the vinegar and minced garlic in a jar. Add salt and pepper to taste. Shake to mix well. While the sweet potato mixture is still slightly warm, gently toss with the vinaigrette. Arrange the lettuce leaves on 4 plates; divide the sweet potato and pineapple mixture among them. Garnish with the green onion and bacon pieces. Serves 4.

Pineapple and Cucumber Salad

1 pineapple, peeled, cored, and cubed
2 cucumbers, peeled and diced
1 tablespoon lemon juice
1/4 cup mayonnaise
Salt and pepper to taste

Toss together the pineapple and cucumber, sprinkle with lemon juice, and blend in the mayonnaise. Add salt and pepper to taste. Serves 4.

Tropical Coleslaw

1 cup fresh pineapple chunks
1/2 head of cabbage, chopped or shredded
1 carrot, grated
1/2 green pepper, diced
1/2 onion, chopped
2 tablespoons rice vinegar
1/2 cup mayonnaise
1 tablespoon prepared mustard
Salt and pepper to taste

Toss together the pineapple, cabbage, carrot, green pepper, and onion. Stir the rice vinegar into the mayonnaise and mustard. Pour the dressing over the slaw and toss well. Season with salt and pepper. Serves 4.

Mexican Salad

Lettuce leaves, enough to line salad platter
1 green bell pepper, cut into strips
1 red bell pepper, cut into strips
1 small red onion, thinly sliced
1 small pineapple, peeled, cored, and cut into chunks
1 large tomato, diced
1 avocado, cut into chunks
Cilantro leaves for garnish
2 tablespoons lime juice
2 tablespoons lemon juice
2 tablespoons chopped cilantro
1/2 teaspoon salt
1/4 cup olive oil
1/4 cup sour cream

Combine the green and red peppers, onion, pineapple, and tomato. Make the dressing by combining all of the remaining ingredients, except for the sour cream, in a jar. Cover and shake well. Then whisk in the sour cream. Pour dressing over salad, toss gently, and then fold in avocado. Mound on lettuce-lined salad platter and garnish with the cilantro leaves. Serves 4.

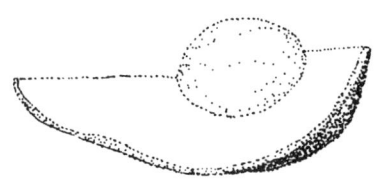

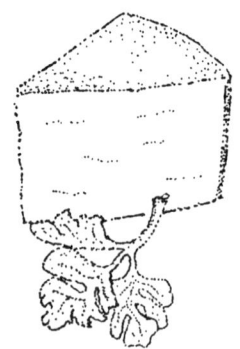

Warm Cheese Salad

Lettuce leaves, torn into bite-sized pieces
1 avocado, cubed
4 fresh pineapple spears
2 tablespoons lemon juice
1 tablespoon prepared mustard
3/4 cup olive oil
1/4 pound Swiss or Jack Cheese

Arrange lettuce leaves on 4 salad plates. Divide the avocado and pineapple among the plates. Combine the lemon juice, mustard, and olive oil in a jar; add salt and pepper to taste. Cover and shake well to mix. Drizzle over salad. Cut the cheese into 2-inch squares and cook in a microwave on a microwave-safe plate (or use ovenproof plate in conventional oven) until soft and melted around the edges. Top the salads with the melted cheese squares and serve. Serves 4.

Nutty Pineapple Rice Salad

2 cups cooked rice
1 tablespoon vegetable oil
1/2 cup orange sections
1/2 cup pineapple chunks
1/2 cup strawberries, sliced
1/4 cup macadamia nuts
2 tablespoons lemon juice
1 tablespoon orange juice
1 teaspoon sugar
1/2 teaspoon dry mustard
Salt and pepper to taste
1/2 cup vegetable oil
2 tablespoons poppy seeds

Blend 1 tablespoon vegetable oil with the cooked rice and cool. Combine the orange sections, pineapple chunks, strawberries, and nuts; then toss with the rice. Whisk together the lemon juice, orange juice, sugar, mustard, salt, and pepper. Then whisk in the oil until thick. Stir in poppy seeds. Pour over the rice salad and serve. Serves 4.

Lentil and Pineapple Salad with Cilantro

1 small pineapple, peeled, cored, and cubed
1-1/2 cups cooked lentils
1 tomato, chopped
1 clove garlic, minced
1 shallot, diced
1 tablespoon white wine vinegar
3 tablespoons olive oil
1/2 teaspoon prepared mustard
1 tablespoon cilantro, minced
Salt and pepper to taste

Combine the pineapple, lentils, and chopped tomato in a salad bowl. Whisk together vinegar, mustard, cilantro, salt, and pepper. Then whisk in the olive oil. Pour the vinaigrette over the salad and serve. Serves 4.

Lentils with Pineapple and Mint

1 cup dried lentils
2 tablespoons olive oil
1/4 teaspoon salt
1/2 cup pineapple tidbits
1 clove garlic, minced
2 tablespoons vinegar
1/2 cup minced red onion
1/4 teaspoon grated orange rind
1/4 cup raisins
1 carrot, minced
1 tablespoon minced parsley
1 tablespoon minced chives
1 tablespoon minced mint

Place lentils in saucepan with enough water to cover. Bring to boil and cover; reduce heat and simmer for 20-30 minutes, until tender. Drain; then rinse in cold water. Add all of the remaining ingredients except for the parsley, chives, and mint. Cover and chill well. Just before serving toss the salad with the parsley, chives, and mint. Serves 4.

Curried Turkey, Pineapple, and Avocado Salad

6 tablespoons mayonnaise
3 tablespoons lemon juice
1-1/2 teaspoons curry powder
2 cups chopped turkey
1 cup fresh pineapple cubes
1/2 cup slivered almonds
2 green onions, chopped
1 stalk celery, sliced
Lettuce leaves
1 avocado, sliced

Mix together the mayonnaise, lemon juice, and curry powder. Add the chopped turkey, pineapple, slivered almonds, green onions and celery. Add salt and pepper to taste. Arrange lettuce leaves on plates and divide the turkey mixture among the plates. Garnish with the sliced avocado. Serves 4.

Pineapple and Chicken Salad

Lettuce leaves
4 poached boneless, skinless chicken breast halves, cubed
1 cup fresh pineapple, cubed
2 stalks celery, diced
1/2 green pepper, diced
1/2 cup mayonnaise
Salt and pepper to taste

Line plates with lettuce leaves. Combine chicken, celery, green pepper, and pineapple. Toss with the mayonnaise and season with salt and pepper. Mound over the lettuce leaves and serve. Serves 4.

Curried Chicken Salad with Pineapple

4 poached boneless, skinless chicken breast halves, cubed
1/2 cup fresh pineapple, cubed
1/4 cup chopped red onion
1 clove garlic, minced
1/4 cup mayonnaise
1 tablespoon curry powder
Lettuce leaves
1 small green pepper, sliced
1 small red pepper, sliced
1 small cucumber, sliced
Sweetened shredded coconut

Combine chicken with pineapple and onion. Mix together mayonnaise, curry powder, and minced garlic. Add to the chicken mixture and toss well. Season to taste with salt and pepper. Chill well. Line 4 salad plates with lettuce leaves. Divide the chicken mixture among the plates and garnish with the peppers and cucumber. Sprinkle coconut over the top and serve. Serves 4.

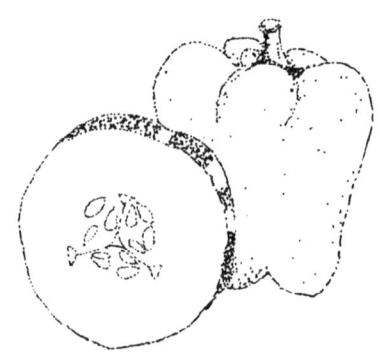

Pineapple Crab Louie

4 cups fresh crabmeat
2 tomatoes, cut into wedges
1 cup fresh pineapple chunks
1 head iceberg lettuce, torn into bite-sized pieces
1/2 cup chili sauce
1/4 cup mayonnaise
1 tablespoon prepared horseradish
Dash cayenne pepper
2 green onions, sliced
2 lemons, cut into wedges

Arrange the crabmeat, tomatoes, and pineapple over the lettuce on individual salad plates. Combine the chili sauce with the mayonnaise, horseradish, and cayenne pepper. Spoon dressing over the salads. Top with the green onions and serve with the lemon wedges. Serves 4.

Martha Ann's Pineapple-Lobster Salad

1 lobster (about 1-1/4 pounds)
1/2 cup celery
1/2 cup diced pineapple
1/4 cup chopped almonds or walnuts
1/4 cup mayonnaise
Cocktail sauce

Immerse the lobster in boiling water, reduce heat and simmer for 5 minutes for the first pound and about 3 minutes for each additional pound. Remove the meat and cut into pieces. Combine the lobster pieces with the celery, pineapple, and nuts. Stir in mayonnaise and serve with cocktail sauce. Serves 2.

Albacore Salad

1 (8-ounce) can crushed pineapple, drained
1 (7-ounce) can albacore tuna, drained
2 green onions, sliced
1/2 red bell pepper, chopped
1/4 cup mayonnaise
1 teaspoon lemon juice
Salt and pepper to taste
1 small head Bibb lettuce

Combine mayonnaise and lemon juice. Add salt and pepper to taste. Mix together the pineapple, tuna, green onions, and red bell pepper. Toss well with the mayonnaise mixture. Arrange over lettuce leaves. Serves 2.

Ahi Stuffed Tomatoes

3/4 pound fresh ahi steaks
1 tablespoon olive oil
3 green onions, sliced
1/4 cup chopped walnuts
12 sliced black olives
1/2 cup pineapple chunks
1/2 cup mayonnaise
Salt and pepper to taste
4 ripe tomatoes, hollowed out

Rub the ahi steaks with the olive oil and bake at 375 degrees for 15 minutes. Chill; then cut into chunks. In a bowl combine the chilled ahi chunks and the remaining ingredients, except the tomatoes. Toss well. Spoon into the hollowed-out tomatoes and serve. Serves 4.

Brunch and Lunch

BRUNCH AND LUNCH

Breakfast Yogurt Hawaiian
Broiled Pineapple with Yogurt
Breakfast Tamales
Pancakes with Fruit Sauce
Pineapple French Toast
Oatmeal with Honeyed Pineapple

Sandwiches
Grilled Breakfast Sandwich
Albacore Salad Sandwich
Ricotta and Pineapple Sandwich
Ham and Cheese Croissant
Canadian Bacon and Pineapple Sandwich
Roast Beef Sandwich
Cheese Quesadillas

Breakfast Yogurt Hawaiian

1 papaya, peeled, seeded, and cubed
1 banana, sliced
1 small pineapple, peeled, cored, and cubed
2 cups plain yogurt
1-1/2 cups granola
1/2 cup chopped nuts (macadamia or pecans)
3 tablespoons honey

Combine fruit. Pour yogurt over fruit and sprinkle with granola and nuts. Drizzle honey over all. Serves 4.

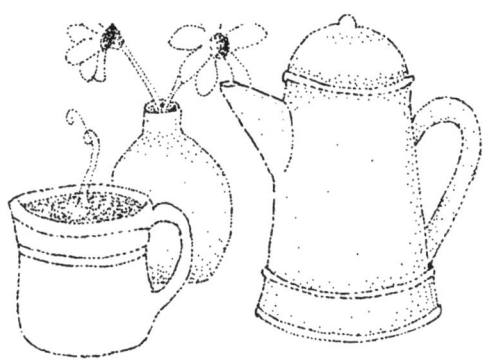

Broiled Pineapple with Yogurt

1 pineapple, peeled, cored, and cut into 1/2" rings
1/2 stick melted butter
1/3 cup honey
1 cup plain yogurt

In buttered baking pan, arrange pineapple rings in one layer. Brush with butter and drizzle with honey. Broil 2 to 3 minutes until bubbly. Serve topped with 2 tablespoons chilled yogurt. Serves 4.

Breakfast Tamales

1 (8-ounce) can crushed pineapple
Water
1 cup instant masa
1/2 teaspoon baking powder
1/4 teaspoon salt
1/3 cup vegetable shortening
1/4 cup brown sugar
8 pieces of foil, 8"x 10" each
1/2 cup diced candied pineapple, cut into small pieces

Drain crushed pineapple, reserving juice. Add enough water to the pineapple juice to make 1 cup. Combine instant masa, baking powder and salt in a medium bowl. Mix in pineapple juice and water mixture. This will form a soft, moist dough. In small bowl beat vegetable shortening until fluffy, add to masa and beat until a small piece of dough floats in a cup of water. Beat in brown sugar and add drained pineapple. Place a rounded tablespoon of dough on each of the foil pieces. Add several pieces of the candied pineapple and top with another tablespoon of dough. Spread to cover the filling and fold foil in half. Fold the edges twice to make a secure seal. On a rack over water in a large pot place the tamales folded side down. Bring water to a boil; then reduce heat to simmer. Cover pot and steam 1 hour. Makes 8 small tamales.

Pancakes with Fruit Sauce

1 (20-ounce) can pineapple chunks, undrained
2 large apples, chopped
2 pears, chopped
1 tablespoon cinnamon
1-1/2 cups flour
1 teaspoon salt
2 teaspoons baking powder
2 eggs, beaten
3 tablespoons melted butter
1 cup milk

Place fruit and cinnamon in a saucepan and cook for 30 minutes over low heat. Sift together flour, salt, and baking powder. Combine beaten eggs, melted butter, and milk, then quickly stir into dry ingredients. Cook pancakes on hot griddle and serve with the fruit sauce. Makes 12 pancakes.

Pineapple French Toast

4 eggs
1 cup pineapple juice
1 tablespoon rum (or vanilla)
8 slices cinnamon raisin bread
Butter
1 tablespoon sugar
Pineapple jam
Coconut syrup

Whisk together eggs, pineapple juice, and rum. Dip the bread into this mixture, coating well. In a large skillet melt the butter. Brown the bread on both sides. Sprinkle with the sugar and serve with pineapple jam and coconut syrup. Serves 4.

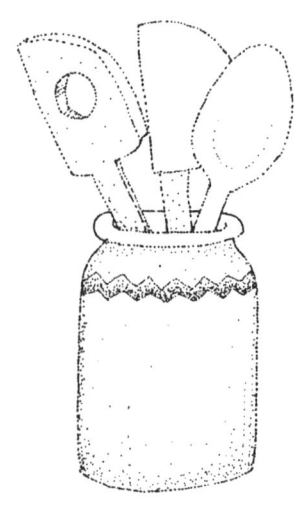

Oatmeal with Honeyed Pineapple

1 tablespoon honey
1 (8-ounce) cup pineapple chunks, undrained
2-2/3 cups water
1-1/3 cups quick oats
1/4 teaspoon cinnamon
1/4 teaspoon nutmeg
1/4 teaspoon salt

Combine juice from pineapple chunks with honey in a saucepan, add pineapple sections, and stir over medium heat for 5 minutes. Meanwhile, make the oatmeal by bringing the water to a boil and adding the oats and spices. Cook 1 minute, remove from heat and let stand covered for 2 minutes. Spoon into bowls and top with the honeyed pineapple. Serves 4.

Grilled Breakfast Sandwich

For two sandwiches:

3 tablespoons pineapple juice
1 egg
4 ounces sliced ham
2 slices Gruyere cheese
4 slices French bread
Butter
1 teaspoon powdered sugar
Pineapple marmalade

Whisk egg and pineapple juice together. Set aside. Divide ham slices and cheese between 2 slices of bread; top with other bread slices. Melt butter in large skillet. Dip each sandwich into the egg mixture, coating well. Cook sandwiches in butter over medium heat until golden. Sprinkle with powdered sugar and serve with the pineapple marmalade. Serves 2.

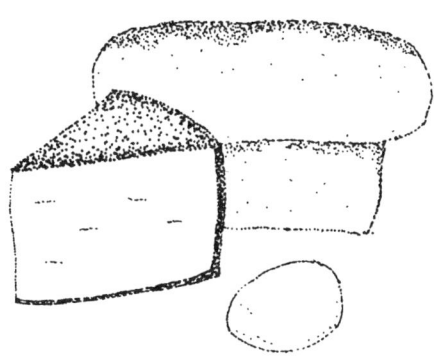

Albacore Salad Sandwich

1 (7-ounce) can albacore tuna, drained
1/4 cup pineapple tidbits, drained
2 tablespoons chopped walnuts
1 green onion, sliced
5 black olives, sliced
3 tablespoons mayonnaise
Sprouts
4 slices whole wheat bread

Combine all ingredients except sprouts and bread. Mix well. Divide mixture between 2 slices of bread; top with sprouts and the other bread slices. Makes 2.

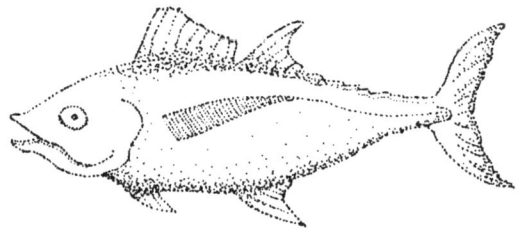

Ricotta and Pineapple Sandwich

1 cup ricotta cheese
1/2 cup pineapple tidbits, well drained
4 slices rye bread
Sprouts

Combine ricotta and pineapple. Spread on 2 slices of bread; top with the sprouts and other slices of bread. Makes 2.

Ham and Cheese Croissant

For each sandwich:

3 ounces thinly sliced ham
2 pineapple rings
1 slice Jack cheese
Freshly baked croissant

Slice open the croissant. Layer ham, pineapple rings, and cheese on one side of the croissant. Broil briefly, until cheese is hot and melted.

Canadian Bacon and Pineapple Sandwich

1 (20-ounce) can pineapple rings, drained
1/4 teaspoon ground ginger
4 tablespoons honey mustard
4 slices Canadian bacon
4 slices Swiss cheese
1 green onion, sliced
8 slices whole wheat bread

Spread honey mustard on 4 slices of bread. Top with Canadian bacon and pineapple slices. Sprinkle with the ground ginger. On other 4 slices of bread layer Swiss cheese sprinkled with the green onion slices. Broil both halves of sandwiches until the cheese is melted. Put sandwiches together and serve. Serves 4.

Roast Beef Sandwich

1/2 cup chopped cabbage
1/4 cup pineapple relish
1/4 cup chopped green onions
6 ounces sliced roast beef
2 sandwich rolls, split

Combine cabbage, pineapple relish, and green onions. Divide roast beef between rolls, top with 1/2 of the cabbage mixture and serve. Makes 2.

Cheese Quesadillas

2 flour tortillas
1 cup grated Jack cheese
4 black olives, sliced
1 avocado, peeled, pitted, and chopped

Divide the cheese and olives between the flour tortillas. Broil until the cheese is hot and melted. Remove from oven and top with the chopped avocado and 2 tablespoons pineappple salsa.

Pineapple Salsa

1 (8-ounce) can pineapple tidbits
1 tablespoon lime juice
3 tablespoons chopped cilantro
1 tablespoon minced jalapeño pepper

Vegetables and Side Dishes

VEGETABLES AND SIDE DISHES

Beets with Pineapple

Gingered Pineapple Broccoli

Almond Carrots with Pineapple

Annie's Green Beans with Pineapple

Sweet Potato Soufflé

Nicole's Rings of Saturn

Martha Ann's Pineapple and Sweet Potatoes

Melodi's Sweet Potatoes

Pineapple Glazed Yams

Marinated Peppers

Pineapple and Apricot Compote

Curried Rice

Brown Rice and Wild Rice

South Seas Baked Beans

Baked Beans with Fruit

Noodles Polynesian

Cheesy Pineapple Casserole

Beets with Pineapple

2 tablespoons brown sugar
1 tablespoon cornstarch
1/4 teaspoon salt
1 (8-ounce) can pineapple chunks in syrup
1 tablespoon butter
1 tablespoon lemon juice
1 (16-ounce) can shoestring beets

Combine brown sugar, cornstarch, and salt in saucepan. Stir in pineapple chunks and syrup. While stirring, heat mixture until it boils and thickens. Stir in butter, lemon juice, and beets. Continue cooking until heated through, about 5 minutes. Serves 4.

Gingered Pineapple Broccoli

2 tablespoons olive oil
1 clove garlic, halved
3/4 pound broccoli, separated into florets, stalks sliced
1 tablespoon vinegar
1/2 cup fresh pineapple chunks
1 tablespoon minced fresh ginger

Sauté garlic in oil for 2 minutes; then discard. Add sliced broccoli stalks; sauté 2 minutes. Add broccoli florets and vinegar and cook for another 3 minutes. Add ginger and pineapple and cook until heated through. Season with salt and pepper to taste. Serves 4.

Almond Carrots with Pineapple

4 medium carrots, sliced
1/2 cup pineapple chunks in juice, drained, juice reserved
2 tablespoons sliced almonds
1 tablespoon butter, melted
2 teaspoons cornstarch
1 tablespoon honey
Salt and pepper to taste

In covered baking dish, layer carrots, pineapple chunks, and sliced almonds. Mix melted butter and cornstarch until smooth. Stir in honey, salt, pepper, and pineapple juice. Pour this mixture over the carrots. Cover casserole and bake for 50 minutes at 400 degrees.

Annie's Green Beans with Pineapple

1 pound green beans, trimmed
1/4 cup crushed pineapple (do not drain)
1 tablespoon brown sugar
2 tablespoons vinegar
1 tablespoon onion, minced
1/2 cup chicken stock
1/4 cup bacon bits

Steam green beans until tender. Combine remaining ingredients in a saucepan. Heat and pour over green beans. Add salt and pepper to taste. Serves 4.

Sweet Potato Soufflé

4 medium sweet potatoes
2 tablespoons butter
1 egg yolk, beaten
Salt
1/2 cup crushed pineapple, drained
1 egg white

Boil potatoes until well done; peel and mash. Beat in butter, the egg yolk and salt to taste. Fold in pineapple. Whip egg white until stiff; then fold into sweet potatoes. Bake in individual buttered soufflé dishes for 20-25 minutes at 350 degrees. Serves 4.

Nicole's Rings of Saturn

This recipe is a favorite of the eight-year-old daughter of a friend. After Mom cooks and mashes the sweet potatoes, it's easy for Nicole to complete the recipe. She tells me that an ice cream scoop is perfect for making the sweet potato balls.

1 (8-ounce) can pineapple rings, drained
2 sweet potatoes, steamed, peeled and mashed
1/4 cup sweetened flaked coconut
2 tablespoons pecans, coarsely chopped

Place pineapple rings on greased cookie sheet. Top each with a scoop of the mashed sweet potatoes. Sprinkle with coconut and pecans. Bake for 15 minutes at 350 degrees.

Martha Ann's Pineapple and Sweet Potatoes

2 pounds sweet potatoes
1/2 cup half and half
3 tablespoons butter
1 (8-ounce) can crushed pineapple, drained
Salt
Marshmallows, split in half

Boil potatoes until well done; peel and mash. While beating potatoes, add half and half, butter, and salt to taste. When potato mixture is fluffy, fold in pineapple. Bake in buttered baking dish for 15 minutes at 350 degrees. Remove from oven and arrange marshmallows on top. Return to oven just long enough for marshmallows to brown and puff. Serves 4-6.

Melodi's Sweet Potatoes

2 medium sweet potatoes
2 tablespoons pineapple juice
1 tablespoon butter, melted
1/4 cup crushed pineapple, drained
1/4 cup shredded coconut
2 tablespoons brown sugar
1/8 teaspoon cinnamon
1/8 teaspoon nutmeg
Salt
2 teaspoons sugar
1/2 cup chopped pecans

Steam potatoes until tender. Cool slightly; then peel and cut into chunks. Mash sweet potatoes; then add pineapple juice and butter. Stir in pineapple, coconut, brown sugar, spices, and salt to taste. Place in well-greased casserole and bake at 375 degrees until lightly browned and bubbly, about 30 minutes. Sprinkle with granulated sugar and pecans; then broil until sugar browns. Serves 4.

Pineapple Glazed Yams

3 yams
3 tablespoons butter
1/4 cup brown sugar
1/2 teaspoon salt
3/4 teaspoon grated orange rind
1 (8-ounce) can crushed pineapple, drained, 2 tablespoons of liquid reserved
2 tablespoons arrowroot
4 tablespoons pecans, chopped

Peel and slice yams about 1/2" thick. Boil for about 10 minutes. In skillet melt butter and add sugar, salt, orange rind, and pineapple. Dissolve the arrowroot in 2 tablespoons of reserved pineapple liquid and stir into pineapple mixture. Add yams and cook until mixture has thickened and yams are quite tender. Sprinkle the pecans over the yams and serve. Serves 4.

Marinated Peppers
Great with calamari.

2 tablespoons olive oil
1 red bell pepper, cut into strips
1 green bell pepper, cut into strips
1 onion, chopped
1/2 cup fresh pineapple chunks
1/4 cup vinegar

Cook pepper strips in olive oil until softened, about 5 minutes. Combine peppers with vinegar and pineapple in bowl; season with salt and pepper to taste. Cover and chill well. Serves 4.

Pineapple and Apricot Compote

3/4 cup honey
2" gingerroot piece, cut into paper-thin slices
4 cups dry white wine
1 pineapple, peeled, cored, and cubed
1 cup dried apricots
1/4 cup dried currants
2 tablespoons lemon juice

In saucepan combine honey, gingerroot slices and wine. Bring to a boil, reduce heat and simmer covered for about 15 minutes, stirring occasionally. Add pineapple and apricots and simmer 5 more minutes. Add currants and simmer 5 minutes more. Transfer fruit to a bowl, leaving gingerroot in syrup. Boil syrup until reduced by half; add lemon juice. Pour syrup over fruit. Serve at room temperature. Serves 4.

Curried Rice

1 medium onion, chopped
2 garlic cloves, minced
2 tablespoons vegetable oil
1-1/3 cups converted rice
1 teaspoon curry
1-1/3 cups chicken broth
2 tablespoons pineapple chutney
1 teaspoon salt

Cook onion and garlic in the oil over medium heat until softened. Add rice and curry powder. Cook, stirring, 2 minutes. Stir in broth, water, chutney, and salt. Bring to a boil, reduce heat, and cook covered over low heat for 20 minutes. Fluff with a fork. Serves 4.

Brown Rice and Wild Rice

1/2 cup onion, chopped
3 tablespoons butter
1 cup brown rice
1 cup wild rice
4 cups water
1/2 cup pineapple tidbits, drained
1/2 red bell pepper, chopped
2 tablespoons minced parsley

Cook onion in the butter over medium heat until it is softened. Stir in wild and brown rice. Cook, stirring, for 2 minutes. Add water and bring to a boil. Reduce heat, cover and simmer 45 minutes. Remove from heat and add pineapple, red bell pepper, and parsley. Add salt and pepper to taste. Serves 4.

South Seas Baked Beans

1 large can baked beans
1 (8-ounce) can pineapple chunks, drained
2 tablespoons brown sugar
2 tablespoons dark rum
Dash of Tabasco

Combine all ingredients in a casserole dish and bake for 30 minutes at 350 degrees.

Baked Beans with Fruit

2 cups canned beans
1/4 teaspoon dry mustard
1 large onion, chopped
1 (8-ounce) can pineapple chunks, drained
1/4 cup honey
Salt

In a casserole dish combine the beans with the mustard, chopped onions, and pineapple chunks. Season with salt to taste. Cover with honey and bake 1 hour at 350 degrees. Serves 4.

Noodles Polynesian

2 tablespoons butter
1/2 cup sliced almonds
1/2 teaspoon cinnamon
1/4 cup raisins
1 tablespoon honey
8 ounces egg noodles
3 eggs, beaten
1/2 teaspoon salt
1 (8-ounce) can crushed pineapple, undrained
1/2 cup bread crumbs
2 tablespoons butter, cut into pieces

Sauté almonds and cinnamon in 2 tablespoons melted butter over medium heat until almonds are toasted. Stir in raisins and honey. Cook for about 3 minutes. Cook the noodles in boiling water until they are almost done. They will finish cooking in the oven. Drain the noodles and transfer to a bowl. Add the almond and raisin mixture, stir, and then add the salt and eggs. Mix well. Stir in pineapple. Spread into a buttered baking dish and top with bread crumbs. Dot top with 2 tablespoons of butter. Bake at 375 degrees for 30 minutes. Serves 4.

Cheesy Pineapple Casserole

1 (20-ounce) can pineapple chunks, drained
1 cup grated Jack cheese
3/4 cup orange juice
1/4 cup honey
1/8 teaspoon salt
1 tablespoon flour
1 cup bread crumbs
1/2 cup diced nuts (macadamia or pecans)
2 tablespoons butter

Combine pineapple and cheese in casserole dish. Mix juice, honey, and salt in saucepan; slowly blend in flour and heat until warm. Pour over pineapple and cheese. Top with bread crumbs and nuts. Dot with butter. Bake 30 minutes at 350 degrees. Serves 4.

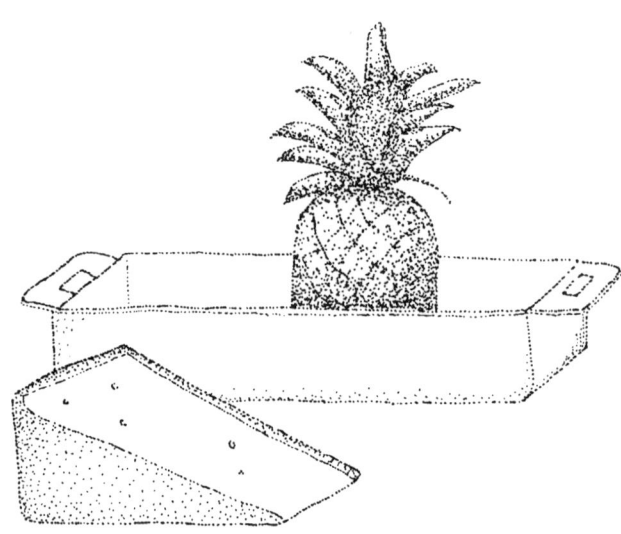

Seafood Poultry and Meats

SEAFOOD, POULTRY, AND MEAT

Seafood
  Shrimp Teriyaki
  Shrimp Tempura
  Grilled Shrimp with Pineapple Relish
  Baked Scallops with Pineapple
  Grilled Scallop Kebabs
  Broiled Ahi Steaks with Fresh Pineapple Relish
  Marinated Swordfish Kebabs

Poultry
  South Seas Barbequed Chicken
  Stuffed Chicken Breasts
  Quick Chicken Roll-Ups
  Chicken with Pineapple and Snow Peas
  Pineapple Chicken
  Chicken and Rice Pineapple Boats
  Michel's Luau Chicken
  Chicken and Pineapple Pasta
  South American Chicken
  Glazed Cornish Game Hens
  Turkey with Macadamia Nuts and Pineapple

Meats
  Pete's Pineapple Steak
  Flank Steak with Pineapple Relish
  Pineapple Stir-Fry
  Maui Meatloaf
  Pineapple Meatballs
  Glazed Roast Loin of Pork
  Roast Pork with Onions and Pineapple
  Puff Pastry Shells with Ham
  Ham Steak Hawaiian
  Glazed Ham

Shrimp Teriyaki

1-1/2 pounds medium raw shrimp
1/2 cup vegetable oil
1/2 cup pineapple juice
1/4 cup soy sauce
2 cloves garlic, minced
1 tablespoon grated fresh ginger

Shell and devein shrimp; then marinate for 15 minutes in the remaining ingredients. Either grill or broil for 3 to 4 minutes on each side. Serves 4.

Shrimp Tempura

2 cups tempura batter mix (follow directions on mix)
1 cup sweetened shredded coconut
16 large raw shrimp, peeled and deveined
Vegetable oil
1 cup pineapple jam
1 tablespoon horseradish

Prepare tempura batter mix according to directions. Dip shrimp into tempura batter; then dredge in coconut. Freeze shrimp on wax-paper-lined baking sheet for 45 minutes. Heat oil in deep skillet and cook shrimp until golden brown, about 3 minutes. Combine pineapple jam and horseradish. Serve with shrimp. Serves 4.

Grilled Shrimp with Pineapple Relish

1 tablespoon vinegar
1/2 cup unsweetened coconut
1 cup fresh pineapple, diced
1 tablespoon minced jalapeño pepper
1/2 red bell pepper, diced
1 small onion, diced
16 large shrimp, peeled and deveined

Combine all ingredients except the shrimp in a bowl. Cover and let stand at room temperature while cooking shrimp. Grill or broil shrimp until pink. Serve with the pineapple mixture. Serves 4.

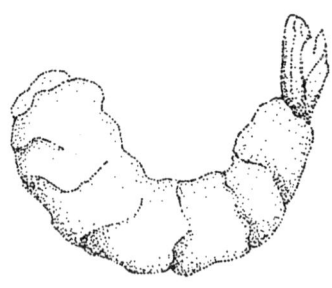

Baked Scallops with Pineapple

1-1/2 pounds sea scallops
1 tablespoon olive oil
1 small can pineapple chunks, drained
1 tablespoon fresh parsley, minced

Place scallops in a baking dish and drizzle with the olive oil. Arrange the pineapple chunks among the scallops and bake until the scallops are cooked, about 10 minutes at 375 degrees. Garnish with parsley and serve. Serves 4.

Grilled Scallop Kebabs

1/2 cup soy sauce
2 tablespoons honey
2 tablespoons dry sherry
1 garlic clove, minced
1-1/2 pounds sea scallops
Bacon strips
1 cup fresh pineapple chunks
1 onion, cut into 3/4-inch squares

Combine first 4 ingredients in small bowl. Clean scallops and wrap 1 slice of bacon around each one. Alternate bacon-wrapped scallops with pineapple chunks and onion pieces on skewers. Grill scallops over moderate heat until golden, basting frequently with sauce. Serves 4.

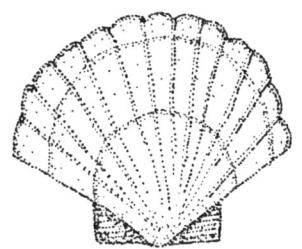

Broiled Ahi Steaks with Fresh Pineapple Relish

4 fresh ahi steaks
1 tablespoon olive oil
1/2 teaspoon dried thyme
Salt and pepper
Lime wedges

Brush tuna steaks with olive oil, sprinkle with thyme, and then salt and pepper to taste. Cook steaks under preheated broiler for 4 to 5 minutes on each side. Serve with Fresh Pineapple Relish.

Fresh Pineapple Relish

1 tablespoon olive oil
1 garlic clove, minced
1-inch piece fresh ginger, minced
1/2 cup chopped macadamia nuts
1-1/2 cups fresh pineapple chunks
2 tablespoons bourbon
Mint leaves for garnish

Sauté garlic in hot oil for 2 minutes, then add ginger and nuts, and cook until nuts are toasted, about 5 minutes. Add pineapple and bourbon and heat to boiling. Remove from heat. Garnish with fresh mint and serve at room temperature. Serves 4.

Marinated Swordfish Kebabs

1-1/2 pounds swordfish, cut into 1-inch cubes
1-1/2 cups fresh pineapple, cut into 1-inch cubes
1 zucchini, cut into 1/2-inch slices
1 red bell pepper, cut into 3/4-inch pieces
1/2 cup Maui Onion Salad Dressing, prepared according to package directions

Marinate swordfish in salad dressing while preparing other ingredients. Alternate swordfish with pineapple, zucchini, and red pepper on skewers. Brush with dressing and grill until swordfish is cooked through, about 10 minutes. Serves 4.

South Seas Barbecued Chicken

1 fresh pineapple
1/4 cup honey
1 can tomato purée
1/4 cup pineapple juice
2 tablespoons vegetable oil
1 tablespoon parsley
1 teaspoon salt
1/8 teaspoon pepper
1 teaspoon chili powder
1 chicken, cut into serving pieces

Remove pineapple crown and cut remainder lengthwise into 8 sections. Core each section but leave the shell on. Brush cut surfaces with honey, wrap in plastic wrap and marinate 1 hour. Combine tomato purée, pineapple juice, oil, parsley, salt, pepper, and chili powder. Grill chicken over hot coals, basting with the tomato sauce. Cook 45 minutes to 1 hour, turning several times and basting frequently with the sauce. Grill pineapple wedges, shell side down, for about 15 minutes. Serve with the chicken. Serves 4.

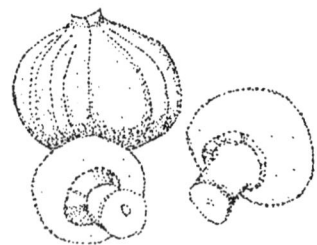

Stuffed Chicken Breasts

4 boneless chicken breasts, flattened
1/4 cup butter
4 thin slices ham
4 small, thin slices Swiss cheese
1 (8-ounce) can pineapple chunks, drained
1 small onion, minced
1 cup sliced mushrooms
1 cup dry white wine
1/2 cup cream
Salt and pepper

Cook chicken breasts in butter until no longer pink. Remove from pan and fold breasts in half over a ham slice, a slice of cheese and a few chunks of pineapple. Keep chicken warm in oven while preparing sauce. In the pan drippings, sauté the onion and mushrooms for 3 or 4 minutes; then add the white wine. Simmer for a few more minutes; then add the cream. Return the chicken breasts to the sauce and heat slowly, turning occasionally. Do not let the sauce boil. Salt and pepper to taste. Serves 4.

Quick Chicken Roll-ups

4 boneless chicken breasts, flattened
4 small, thin slices of cheese (Mozzarella or Swiss)
4 fresh pineapple spears
1 cup flour
2 eggs, beaten
1/2 cup bread crumbs

Flatten chicken breasts; then place 1 slice of cheese and 1 pineapple spear on each. Roll each chicken breast, totally enclosing cheese and pineapple; secure with a toothpick if necessary. Roll in flour, dip into beaten egg and coat with bread crumbs. Deep fry until golden. Drain on paper towels. Serves 4.

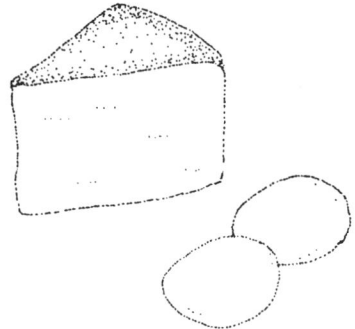

Chicken with Pineapple and Snow Peas

1/2 ounce dried shiitake mushrooms
2 large chicken breasts, boned and cut into cubes
1/4 cup flour
2 tablespoons butter
1 onion, chopped
1 clove garlic, chopped
1 (8-ounce) can pineapple chunks, drained and juice reserved
1 tablespoon tomato paste
1 cup chicken broth
1 dash cayenne pepper
Salt and pepper
1 cup snow peas

Rinse the shiitake mushrooms, barely cover with warm water and soak for 20 minutes. Then strain (reserving mushroom liquid) and cut into pieces. Dredge the chicken cubes in flour and brown in butter. Add the chopped onion and garlic and cook for 3 minutes. Add reserved pineapple juice, tomato paste, mushroom liquid and chicken broth. Stir in mushrooms. Cover and simmer until almost completely cooked. Remove cover and reduce sauce. Add cayenne and season with salt and pepper to taste. Add pineapple chunks and snow peas. Cover and simmer 10 minutes. Serve with rice. Serves 4.

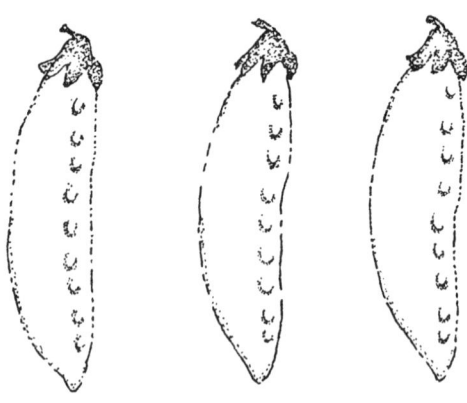

Pineapple Chicken

1 chicken, cut into serving pieces
Juice and peel of 1 lime
Salt and pepper
2 tablespoons butter
2 medium onions, chopped
1 large tomato, chopped
2 tablespoons raisins
1/4 teaspoon Tabasco sauce
1 clove garlic, crushed
1 cup chicken broth
1 (20-ounce) can pineapple rings

Marinate chicken in the lime juice, a few strips of the lime peel, and salt and pepper to taste for at least one hour, turning often. Drain the chicken; then brown in the butter. Add the chopped onion, tomato, raisins, Tabasco sauce, and garlic to the chicken. Cook for 5 minutes. Add the chicken broth and cover and cook until tender. Remove chicken to a serving platter. Pour off fat and add pineapple rings. Bring to a hard boil to reduce sauce. Serve sauce with pineapple, chicken, and rice. Serves 4.

Chicken and Rice Pineapple Boats

1 cup wild rice
4 boned chicken breasts
1/4 cup flour
4 tablespoons butter
1 minced green pepper
2 cups condensed cream of mushroom soup
1/2 cup milk
4 tablespoons dry sherry
2 pineapples

Wash the wild rice well; then stir it slowly into 4 cups of boiling water and 1 teaspoon salt. Cook for about 35 minutes or until tender. Dredge the chicken breasts in the flour and sauté in the butter until done. Remove the chicken breasts from the pan and keep warm. Add the green pepper to the pan drippings and sauté until tender. Stir in the condensed soup and milk and heat slowly. Add the sherry. Split the pineapples lengthwise and create a cavity by removing the core and some of the flesh. Heat the pineapple shells by briefly dipping them into boiling water. Fill each pineapple cavity with 1/4 of the rice and a chicken breast. Spoon some of the sauce over each. Serves 4.

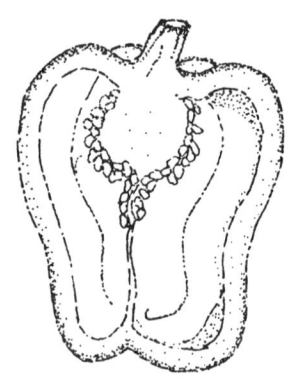

Michel's Luau Chicken

Michel told me he made this dish to impress his dates with his cooking ability, but not to tell anybody how really easy it is to make.

Meat from 1 whole cooked chicken, cubed
1 fresh pineapple, halved lengthwise
1 (10-ounce) can raspberry or strawberry or cranberry applesauce

Scoop out pineapple flesh and chop. Mix with chicken meat and the raspberry, strawberry or cranberry applesauce. Refill the pineapple shells and bake until heated. Serves 2.

Chicken and Pineapple Pasta

1 pound whole-wheat pasta (soba)
1/4 cup sesame oil
1/4 cup soy sauce
1-1/2 tablespoons rice vinegar
1 teaspoon hot pepper oil
1/4 cup thinly sliced green onions
2 boneless chicken breasts, sliced
2 tablespoons peanut oil
1 red bell pepper, julienned
2 small Japanese eggplants, cubed
1 clove garlic, minced
1 small can pineapple chunks

Cook pasta in boiling water until tender, 8 to 10 minutes. Drain. Combine next 5 ingredients in jar; cover and shake. Pour over noodles and toss well. Sauté the chicken in the peanut oil until no longer pink. Add the red pepper, eggplant, and garlic and cook until the pepper is soft. Add the pineapple and cook 3 - 5 minutes more. Add the vegetables and chicken to the noodles and toss. Serves 4.

South American Chicken

1 whole chicken, cut into pieces
2 tablespoons olive oil
4 medium potatoes, cubed
1 large onion, sliced
1 8-ounce can pineapple chunks (do not drain)
3/4 cup sliced black olives
1 cup water

Brown chicken in hot olive oil over medium heat. Add remaining ingredients, cover, and cook until the chicken is tender, about 30 minutes. Remove cover and continue cooking for another 10 minutes. Serves 4.

Glazed Cornish Game Hens

2 1-1/4-pound Cornish hens
2 tablespoons melted butter
2 tablespoons water
1/2 cup pineapple jam
1 tablespoon prepared mustard
1/2 teaspoon rosemary
Dash cayenne pepper
1 clove garlic, minced

Preheat oven to 450 degrees. Place Cornish hens breast-side-up in a roasting pan. Brush with melted butter. Reduce heat to 350 degrees and roast uncovered for 30 minutes. Combine remaining ingredients. Coat the hens with the thick glaze and continue roasting for 15 minutes more. Split hens in half and serve. Serves 4.

Turkey with Macadamia Nuts and Pineapple

1 pound turkey breast, sliced
Flour, seasoned with salt and pepper
2 eggs, beaten
1-1/2 cups bread crumbs
3/4 cup finely chopped macadamia nuts
1 (8-ounce) can pineapple rings, cut in halves
2 tablespoons butter
2 tablespoons vegetable oil
1/2 cup orange juice
1 cup chicken stock
1/2 teaspoon cornstarch
2 tablespoons bourbon

Dredge turkey in flour mixture, dip in eggs and then coat with a combination of the bread crumbs and the macadamia nuts. Cook the turkey in the butter and vegetable oil over moderate heat for 2 minutes on each side. After all of the turkey is cooked, briefly sauté the pineapple rings in the same pan. Keep the turkey and pineapple rings warm. Wipe out the pan and add the orange juice and chicken stock. Boil until reduced by half. In a small bowl whisk together the cornstarch and bourbon. Add to the sauce mixture, salt and pepper to taste, and then bring to a boil. Arrange the turkey and pineapple rings on a platter and spoon sauce over turkey. Serves 4.

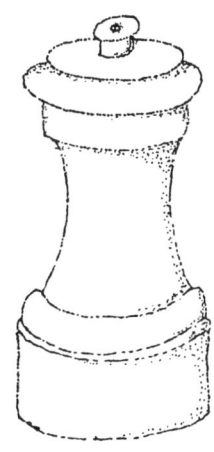

Pete's Pineapple Steak

1 pound boneless round steak
1/2 teaspoon pepper
1 garlic clove, minced
2 teaspoons chili powder
2 tablespoons oil
3 green onions, sliced
1 carrot, sliced
2 celery stalks, sliced
1 (20-ounce) can sliced pineapple, drained and juice reserved
3/4 cup reserved pineapple juice
1 15-ounce can tomato sauce

Trim fat from steak; cut steak into cubes. Place between 2 sheets of plastic wrap and flatten with mallet or rolling pin until 1/4" thick. Sprinkle steak with pepper, garlic, and chili powder. Heat oil in skillet, add steak and brown on both sides. Remove steak from skillet and add green onions, carrots, and celery. Sauté over medium heat for 5 minutes. Return steak to skillet and add reserved pineapple juice and tomato sauce. Cover, reduce heat and simmer 1-1/2 hours or until tender. Cut all but 4 of the pineapple rings into chunks and add to the steak mixture. Cook 5 minutes. Serve garnished with remaining pineapple rings. Serves 4.

Flank Steak with Pineapple Relish

1/2 cup pineapple juice
1/4 cup red wine
2 teaspoons honey
2 teaspoons prepared mustard
1 (8-ounce) can pineapple tidbits (do not drain)
2 green onions, chopped
1/2 cup water
2 tablespoons sugar
1/4 teaspoon dry mustard
2 tablespoons minced cilantro
1-1/2 pounds lean flank steak

Combine pineapple juice, wine, honey and mustard. Marinate flank steak in mixture overnight. In small saucepan combine pineapple tidbits, green onions, water, sugar and mustard. Bring to a boil, reduce heat and simmer 30 minutes, stirring occasionally. Cool to room temperature; then stir in cilantro. Remove steak from the marinade and broil 4 inches from heat to desired degree of doneness, basting with the marinade. Slice steak across grain into thin slices. Serve with pineapple mixture. Serves 4-5.

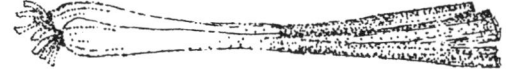

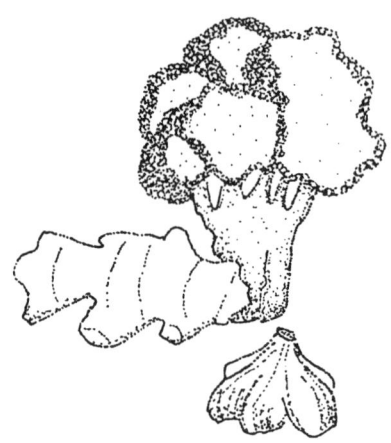

Pineapple Stir-Fry

1/2 cup pineapple juice
1/4 cup soy sauce
2 cloves garlic, minced
2 teaspoons sesame oil
2 tablespoons cornstarch
1 pound flank steak
2 tablespoons vegetable oil
1 tablespoon fresh ginger, minced
1 pound broccoli, cut into florets
1/2 cup chicken broth
1 pound mushrooms
1 (8-ounce) can pineapple chunks

Combine first 5 ingredients. Stir to dissolve cornstarch. Thinly slice beef across grain into strips. Heat 1 tablespoon oil in wok or large skillet over high heat. Add beef and sauté until no longer pink. Transfer to platter. Add remaining tablespoon of oil to wok or skillet. Add ginger, sauté for about 30 seconds, and then add the broccoli. Sauté 1 minute; then add the chicken broth. Cover, reduce heat and simmer about 2 minutes. Add mushrooms; cover and cook until broccoli is crisp-tender. Return beef to wok, stir sauce and add to wok. Add pineapple chunks and cook until sauce has thickened. Serve with freshly cooked rice. Serves 4.

Maui Meatloaf

You'll need one 8-ounce can of crushed pineapple for this recipe. Half of the pineapple is used in the meatloaf, and all of the liquid and the other half of the pineapple are used in the sauce.

Meatloaf:

1/2 cup canned crushed pineapple, liquid reserved
2 pounds lean ground beef
1 onion, chopped
1 tablespoon soy sauce
1 clove garlic, minced
Salt and pepper to taste

Sauce:

1/2 cup crushed pineapple
Reserved pineapple liquid
3 green onions, chopped
3 tablespoons tomato paste
1 tablespoon soy sauce
2 tablespoons lemon juice
1 tablespoon brown sugar
1/8 teaspoon ginger

Drain the pineapple, reserving the liquid. Combine 1/2 cup drained pineapple, ground beef, onion, soy sauce, garlic, salt, and pepper. Press into a one-quart loaf pan. Bake at 350 degrees for 45 minutes. Combine all the sauce ingredients in a small saucepan and heat thoroughly. Spoon over meatloaf. Serves 4.

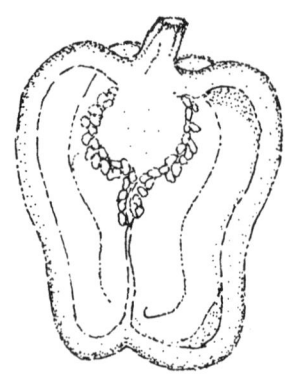

Pineapple Meatballs

1 pound ground sirloin
1/2 pound ground beef
1-1/4 cups seasoned Italian breadcrumbs
2 eggs
1/3 cup cold water

Mix all ingredients. Shape into 2-1/2" balls. Place 1/2" apart in greased baking pan. Bake at 350 degrees for 35 minutes. Layer in serving dish and cover with pineapple sauce.

Pineapple Sauce:

3 celery stalks, sliced
1/2 bell pepper, chopped
1 (20-ounce) can pineapple chunks, drained
2 cups pineapple juice
1/2 cup brown sugar
1/4 cup white wine
1/4 cup vinegar
2 tablespoons cornstarch

In a saucepan dissolve the cornstarch in the vinegar and then add the pineapple juice, brown sugar, and white wine. Cook over low heat until clear. Stir in celery, pepper, and pineapple. Pour over the meatballs and serve.

Glazed Roast Loin of Pork

1 teaspoon thyme
1 teaspoon dry mustard
Salt and pepper to taste
1 3-1/2-pound pork loin roast
1 cup pineapple jam
1 tablespoon soy sauce
2 tablespoons dry sherry

Combine thyme, mustard, salt, and pepper. Rub over surface of pork roast. Place roast, fat side up, on rack in roasting pan. Roast at 425 degrees for 3/4 to 2 hours. In small saucepan heat pineapple jam, soy sauce, and dry sherry. Reduce sauce over low heat, stirring constantly. Remove roast from oven and cool at room temperature. Spoon glaze over roast and serve.

Roast Pork with Onions and Pineapple

1 3-1/2-pound loin of pork
Salt and pepper
2 cloves garlic, minced
2 teaspoons crushed rosemary
1 (8-ounce) can pineapple chunks, drained
1/2 cup cognac
1/2 cup dry white wine
10 small onions, peeled and left whole
2 tablespoons butter

Rub the pork with salt, pepper, garlic, and rosemary. Roast in a 425-degree oven for 1-3/4 to 2 hours. Soak pineapple in the cognac at least 30 minutes. Remove the roast from the pan and add the wine, scraping up any bits of cooked pork, and pour into a small saucepan. Reduce by 1/2 over high heat. Sauté the small onions in the butter until browned, about 5 minutes. Add the reduced pan drippings and the pineapple and cognac. Heat thoroughly. Serve the pork roast with the onion and pineapple sauce. Serves 4.

Puff Pastry Shells with Ham

4 puff pastry shells, defrosted and heated according to package directions (or 4 slit and toasted English muffins)
3 tablespoons butter
1 small onion, chopped
1 cup cooked ham, chopped
1/4 cup black olives, sliced
1/2 cup pineapple chunks, drained
Salt and pepper to taste
Pinch of cayenne pepper
2 tablespoons parsley
1 egg yolk, beaten
1/2 cup heavy cream

In skillet sauté onion in the butter until tender. Add the ham, black olives, and pineapple chunks. Stir, and then add cayenne, parsley, salt, and pepper. Mix beaten egg yolk into cream; then add to the ham and pineapple mixture. Cook until thickened but don't allow it to boil. Fill warm pastry shells or pour over toasted English muffins. Serves 4.

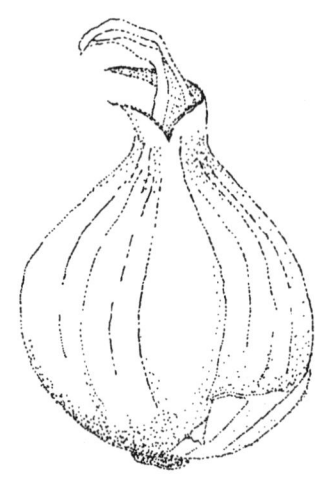

Ham Steak Hawaiian

1 ham steak
1 tablespoon butter
1 (8-ounce) can pineapple chunks
2 tablespoons Madeira
Pineapple juice
1 tablespoon brown sugar
1 teaspoon cinnamon
Hot mustard (optional)

Using an ovenproof skillet, sauté ham steak in butter. After browning on one side, turn the ham steak over and place the pineapple on top. Add the Madeira. Bake the ham steak at 350 degrees for 30 minutes, basting occasionally with pineapple juice. Mix the brown sugar with the cinnamon and sprinkle over the pineapple. Broil briefly until glaze bubbles. May be served with hot mustard.

Glazed Ham

1 14-16-pound cooked ham, bone in
Whole cloves
16 ounces beer
1 tablespoon minced fresh ginger
1/2 cup bourbon
1/2 cup pineapple jam
2 tablespoons prepared mustard
1/4 cup brown sugar

Prepare ham for roasting. Cut diagonal lines in fat layer to create a diamond pattern. Press 1 clove into each diamond. Place ham in a roasting pan. Combine the beer and ginger and pour over the ham. Bake ham for 10 minutes per pound at 350 degrees, basting every 15 minutes. Meanwhile, in small saucepan combine the bourbon, pineapple jam, and mustard. Heat until warm, about 5 minutes. Thirty minutes before ham completes baking, remove from oven, brush glaze over ham and sprinkle with brown sugar. Increase oven temperature to 450 degrees and complete baking. Transfer ham to serving platter and serve.

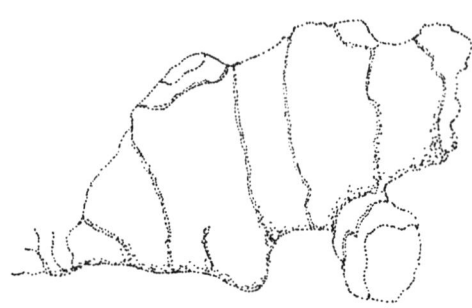

Muffins and Breads

MUFFINS AND BREADS

Martha Ann's Pineapple Muffins
Broiled Pineapple Toast
Nutty Pineapple Muffins
Pineapple Upside-Down Muffins
Oat Bran Muffins
Pineapple Oat Bran Bread
Pineapple Crescents

Martha Ann's Pineapple Muffins

2 eggs
2 teaspoons sugar
1 cup milk
2 cups flour
1/2 teaspoon salt
3 teaspoons baking powder
2 tablespoons vegetable oil
1/2 cup crushed pineapple, drained

Beat eggs; add sugar. Then beat in milk and sifted flour, salt, and baking powder. Stir in oil and pineapple. Bake in greased muffin tins at 375 degrees for 20 minutes.

Broiled Pineapple Toast

2 tablespoons pineapple juice
1/4 cup sugar
4 slices bread
Butter

Combine the pineapple juice and sugar. Toast and butter the bread. Spread the bread with the pineapple mixture. Then brown the top lightly under the broiler. Serves 2.

Nutty Pineapple Muffins

2 cups whole wheat flour
1 teaspoon baking soda
1/4 teaspoon baking powder
1/2 teaspoon salt
2 eggs, separated
2 tablespoons melted butter
2 tablespoons honey
1 cup buttermilk
1/2 cup crushed pineapple, undrained
1/2 cup chopped walnuts

Combine flour, baking soda, baking powder, and salt. Beat the egg whites until stiff. Then mix the melted butter with the honey, buttermilk, pineapple, walnuts, and egg yolks. Mix well. Combine with the flour mixture; then fold in the beaten egg whites. Fill well-oiled muffin pans 2/3 full and bake at 375 degrees for 20 minutes.

Optional Frosting:

Blend 6 ounces of whipped cream cheese with 1/2 cup crushed pineapple. Spread over cooled muffins. Sprinkle with chopped nuts.

Pineapple Upside-Down Muffins

1/3 cup butter
1/3 cup maple syrup
1 (8-ounce) can pineapple rings, cut into quarters
1 cup bran
1/2 cup chopped pecans
1/2 cup whole wheat flour
2 tablespoons brown sugar
1 teaspoon baking soda
1/4 teaspoon salt
3/4 cup buttermilk
6 tablespoons maple syrup
1/4 cup butter, melted
2 large eggs

Butter 10 muffin cups. Melt 1/3 cup butter with 1/3 cup maple syrup in saucepan. Pour into bottoms of prepared cups. Place a quarter of a pineapple ring in the bottom of each cup. Mix bran with the next 6 ingredients. Stir in buttermilk, maple syrup, melted butter, and eggs. Add to dry ingredients and mix just until combined. Fill muffin cups and bake at 400 degrees for about 30 minutes.

Oat Bran Muffins

1 cup whole wheat flour
1 cup oat bran
1 teaspoon baking soda
1 teaspoon baking powder
1/2 teaspoon salt
1 teaspoon cinnamon
1/4 cup honey
2 eggs, well beaten
1/2 cup brown sugar
2/3 cup vegetable oil
1 cup grated carrots
1/2 cup crushed pineapple

Sift together whole wheat flour, oat bran, baking soda, baking powder, salt, and cinnamon. Add the honey, eggs, brown sugar, and oil. Mix well. Then stir in the grated carrots and crushed pineapple. Pour into well-oiled muffin pans or use paper liners. Fill muffin tins about 2/3 full. Bake 20-25 minutes at 375 degrees. Makes about 1 dozen muffins.

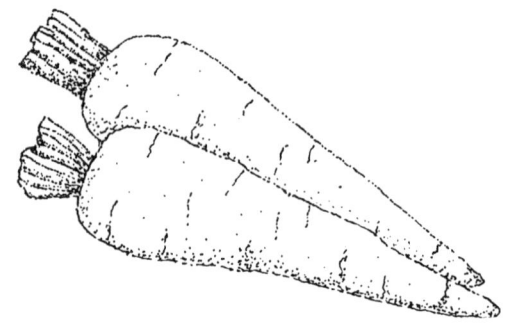

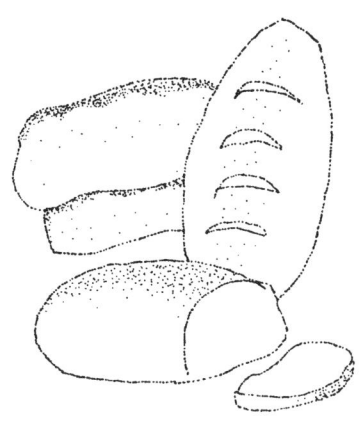

Pineapple Oat Bran Bread

1-1/2 cups oat bran
1 cup unbleached flour
1/4 teaspoon cinnamon
1 teaspoon baking powder
3/4 teaspoon baking soda
1/2 teaspoon salt
1/4 teaspoon nutmeg
1/4 cup raisins
1/2 cup pineapple juice
1/2 cup buttermilk
3 tablespoons honey
2 eggs
2 tablespoons vegetable oil
1 teaspoon vanilla extract
3/4 cup pineapple tidbits

Combine the oat bran, flour, cinnamon, baking powder, baking soda, salt, and nutmeg. Stir in raisins. Whisk together the pineapple juice, buttermilk, honey, eggs, oil, and vanilla. Add the pineapple. Combine with the dry ingredients. Pour into a greased 8-inch square pan and bake at 375 degrees for 35 minutes. Let cake cool in pan, run knife around edges and then invert onto a cooling rack. Good with yogurt or ricotta cheese. Serves 8.

Pineapple Crescents

4 ounces cream cheese, softened
2 tablespoons sugar
1/8 teaspoon nutmeg
1/8 teaspoon cinnamon
1 (8-ounce) can crushed pineapple, drained
1 package refrigerated crescent rolls
Powdered sugar

Combine cream cheese, sugar, and spices. Stir in pineapple. Unroll crescent roll dough and separate into triangles. Spread about 1-1/2 tablespoons of pineapple mixture on each triangle. Loosely roll up triangles, bend into crescent shape and place seam side down on a baking sheet. Bake about 15 minutes at 375 degrees. Remove from baking sheet and dust with powdered sugar. Makes 8.

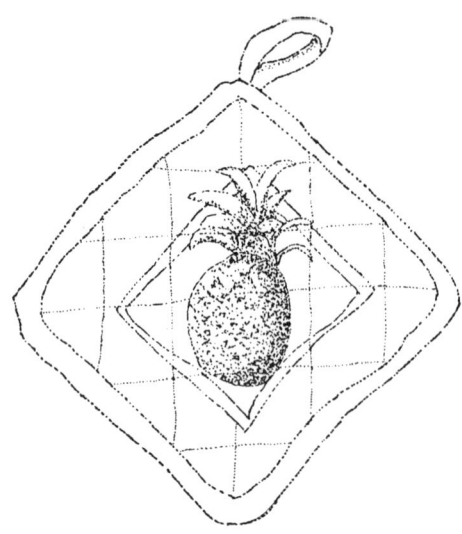

Desserts

DESSERTS

Pies and Pastries
  Honolua Pie
  Pineapple and Apricot Pie
  Melodi's Coconut Pineapple Pie
  Pineapple Tart
  Cinnamon Pineapple Turnovers

Cakes and Cookies
  Pineapple Cheesecake
  Pineapple Pecan Upside-Down Cake
  Eleanor's Upside-Down Cake
  Walnut Carrot Cake with Pineapple
  Pineapple-Glazed Sponge Cake
  Cinnamon Pineapple Cookies

Fruit Desserts
  Pineapple with Bourbon Cream
  Pineapple and Bananas with Cream
  Gingered Cream over Pineapple
  Molded Pineapple Cream Cheese
  Brandied Pineapple
  Glazed Pineapple
  Fresh Pineapple in Pineapple Wine
  Pineapple Flambé
  Fruit Fondue
  Baked Rhubard and Pineapple
  Bread Pudding
  Pineapple Custard Crisps
  Rice Pudding
  Pineapple Tapioca Pudding

Frozen Desserts
  Pineapple Sorbet
  Pineapple-Lime Sorbet

Honolua Pie

1 (20-ounce) can pineapple chunks, drained
Pastry for 1 double-crust 8-inch pie
1/2 cup sugar
1 tablespoon cornstarch
1/8 teaspoon salt
1 tablespoon butter, cut into pieces
1/8 teaspoon cinnamon
1 tablespoon milk
1-1/2 tablespoons sugar

Preheat oven to 425 degrees. Prepare pastry. Line an 8-inch pie plate with 1/2 of the pastry. Arrange the drained pineapple evenly in pastry shell. Blend together 1/2 cup sugar, cornstarch and salt. Sprinkle evenly over the pineapple. Dot with butter and sprinkle with cinnamon. Top with the remaining half of the pastry. Seal edges. Cut slits in top and brush pie with milk and sprinkle with sugar. Lower heat to 350 degrees and bake for 45 minutes. Makes 1 8-inch pie.

Pineapple and Apricot Pie

Pastry:

1 cup flour
6 tablespoons butter
2 tablespoons sugar
1 egg yolk
1 tablespoon liquid from canned pineapple
1/4 teaspoon salt

Pie Filling:

1 cup apricot preserves
3 tablespoons bourbon
1 (20-ounce) can sliced pineapples
1 (20-ounce) can apricot halves
1 cup whipped cream

For pastry: Put flour in a food processor, add other ingredients and process until a smooth ball forms. Chill while preparing apricot glaze; then roll out and fit into an 8-inch pie pan. Weight bottom of pie shell with uncooked rice or beans and bake at 400 degrees until lightly browned, about 15 minutes. For filling: Cook preserves in small saucepan for about 4 minutes; then stir in bourbon. Brush the cooked pie shell with 2 tablespoons of the apricot glaze. Then arrange the pineapple slices over the glaze and add the apricot halves. Cover the top of the pie with the remaining apricot glaze. Serve topped with the whipped cream.

Melodi's Coconut Pineapple Pie

1/2 cup butter
1-1/2 cups sugar
2 tablespoons flour
2 eggs, beaten
2 teaspoons vanilla
1 (8-ounce) can crushed pineapple
4 ounces sweetened flaked coconut
1 9-inch pie shell

Beat butter with sugar until smooth; add remaining ingredients. Pour into unbaked pie shell and bake at 350 degrees for 45 minutes.

Pineapple Tart

8" pie shell
1 fresh pineapple, peeled, cored, and cubed
3/4 teaspoon cinnamon
1 tablesoon butter
1 tablespoon sugar
1/2 cup Madeira
1/2 cup water
1 cup heavy whipping cream

While pie shell is baking, cook pineapple, cinnamon, butter, and sugar in Madeira and water until the pineapple is golden brown. Pour into hot pastry shell. Stir in whipping cream. Serve chilled.

Cinnamon Pineapple Turnovers

1 (20-ounce) can pineapple chunks, drained
1/4 cup sugar
1 tablespoon flour
1/2 teaspoon cinnamon
1/8 teaspoon nutmeg
1/8 teaspoon salt
6 sheets frozen phyllo pastry, thawed
Melted butter

Combine pineapple chunks, sugar, flour, cinnamon, nutmeg and salt. Cut each phyllo sheet lengthwise into 4 strips. Brush each strip with melted butter. Stack two strips, one on top of the other. Then spread 1 tablespoon of pineapple mixture over each double-thickness strip within one inch of one end. Starting at other end, fold bottom left corner over mixture, forming a triangle. Continue folding back and forth, forming triangles until you reach the end of the strip. Repeat with remaining pineapple filling and sheets of phyllo dough. Place seam side down on buttered baking sheet. Bake at 400 degrees for about 15 minutes, until golden. Makes 24 small turnovers.

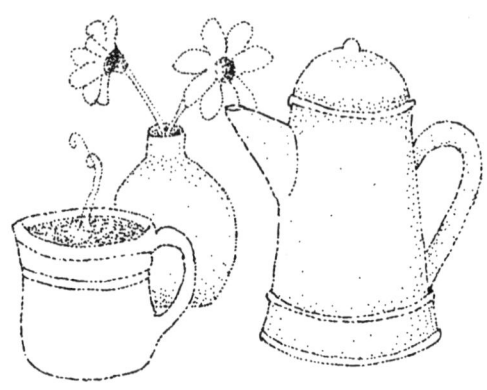

Pineapple Cheesecake

Crust:

1-1/2 cups graham cracker crumbs
1/4 cup sugar
6 tablespoons butter

Filling:

24 ounces cream cheese
1-1/4 cups sugar
6 eggs, separated
1 pint sour cream
1/3 cup flour
2 teaspoons vanilla extract
1 (8-ounce) can pineapple rings, cut up

Mix the crumbs with the sugar and butter; then line the bottom and sides of a 10-inch springform pan. Beat the cream cheese and sugar until soft and creamy. Beat in egg yolks one at a time. Stir in sour cream, flour, vanilla and pineapple pieces. Beat the egg whites until stiff and fold into the cheese mixture. Pour the cheese mixture into the graham cracker crust and bake in preheated oven at 350 degrees for 1 hour. Turn off the heat, open the oven door slightly and allow the cheesecake to remain in the oven for another hour. Chill overnight before serving.

Pineapple Pecan Upside-Down Cake

1 (20-ounce) can sliced pineapple in syrup, 1/4 cup syrup reserved
4 tablespoons butter
1/3 cup brown sugar
1/4 cup pecans
1 egg
1/2 cup granulated sugar
1-1/2 cups all-purpose flour
2 teasoons baking powder
1/4 teaspoon salt
1/2 cup milk
2 teaspoons vanilla extract

Drain pineapple, reserving syrup. Melt the butter in a small saucepan, reserving two tablespoons. Add the brown sugar to the saucepan. Cook over low heat for 1 minute, stirring constantly. Add pineapple syrup and cook 1 minute more. Spread evenly in an 8-inch round pan. Arrange the pineapple slices over the brown sugar mixture, covering the bottom of the pan. Cut the extra pineapple slices in half and stand on edge at the sides of the pan. Sprinkle the nuts between the pineapple slices. Beat the egg until foamy; gradually add the sugar and the reserved 2 tablespoons of butter. Beat well. Combine sifted flour, baking powder and salt. Add the flour mixture to the egg alternately with the milk. Mix well after each addition. Stir in vanilla. Pour the batter over the pineapple slices. Bake at 350 degrees for about 45 minutes. Cool in pan; then invert onto serving platter.

Eleanor's Upside-Down Cake

1 fresh pineapple, peeled, cored, and sliced
1/2 cup hazelnuts
1/2 cup butter, melted
1/2 cup brown sugar
1 cup butter, softened
4 eggs
1 cup sugar
1-1/2 cups flour
2 teaspoons baking powder
1 teaspoon ground ginger
1/2 cup ground hazelnuts
1/4 cup pineapple juice

Cover bottom and sides of cake pan with the combined melted butter and 1/2 cup of brown sugar. Place pineapple rings over butter and sugar mixture in an attractive design. Cut rings in half for pan sides. Distribute hazelnuts around pineapple. Beat together remaining ingredients and spread evenly over the pineapple. Bake at 350 degrees for 50 minutes.

Walnut Carrot Cake with Pineapple

1 cup vegetable oil
1 cup sugar
1 cup firmly packed brown sugar
4 eggs
1 cup all purpose flour
1 cup whole wheat flour
2 teaspoons cinnamon
2 teaspoons baking soda
1 teaspoon baking powder
1 teaspoon vanilla
2 cups grated carrots
1 (8-ounce) can crushed pineapple, drained, 2 tablespoons liquid reserved
3/4 cup chopped walnuts

Preheat oven to 350 degrees. Butter a 9- x 13-inch baking pan. Using electric mixer, combine first 4 ingredients in large bowl. Sift together both flours, cinnamon, baking soda, and baking powder. Mix into liquid ingredients. Stir in vanilla, carrots, pineapple with reserved juice and walnuts. Pour into prepared pan. Bake until a tester comes out clean, about 45 minutes. Cool.

Cream Cheese Frosting (optional)

1 6-ounce package cream cheese, room temperature
2 tablespoons butter, room temperature
1 teaspoon vanilla
3/4 cup powdered sugar
2 tablespoons milk

Using electric mixer, combine cream cheese, butter and vanilla. Beat in the sugar alternately with the milk. Spread on cake.

Pineapple-Glazed Sponge Cake

1 cup cake flour
1 cup sugar
1/4 teaspoon salt
1 teaspoon baking powder
6 egg yolks
1/4 cup pineapple juice
6 egg whites
1/2 cup sugar

Pineapple Glaze:

1 cup pineapple jam
4 tablespoons bourbon

Sift together the flour, 1 cup sugar, salt, and baking powder. Beat in the egg yolks and the pineapple juice. Beat the egg whites until fluffy, add the 1/2 cup sugar and continue beating until stiff peaks form. Fold the egg whites into the flour and egg yolk mixture. Pour into an ungreased 10-inch tube pan. Bake at 350 degrees for 45 minutes. Cool cake in its pan; then unmold. While cake is cooling, prepare the pineapple glaze: Heat 1 cup pineapple jam in small saucepan. Stir in 4 tablespoons bourbon. Pour warm glaze over the cake and serve.

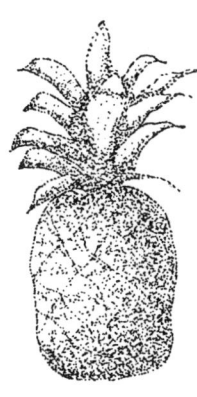

Cinnamon Pineapple Cookies

3/4 stick butter, softened
6 tablespoons brown sugar
1 egg
1/2 teaspoon vanilla extract
3/4 cup flour
1/2 teaspoon baking powder
1/4 teaspoon salt
1-1/2 cups quick-cooking oats
3 tablespoons pineapple juice
1/2 teaspoon cinnamon
1/2 cup pineapple tidbits, well drained

Cream butter and sugar together and beat in the egg and vanilla. Sift together the flour, baking powder, and salt. Stir flour mixture into the batter; then add remaining ingredients. Combine well. Drop by rounded teaspoonfuls onto greased cookie sheets. Flatten slightly. Bake for 12 - 15 minutes at 350 degrees. Makes 2 dozen cookies.

Pineapple with Bourbon Cream

1 cup whipping cream
2 tablespoons bourbon
1/2 cup pineapple jam

Whip the cream until stiff peaks form. Stir in the bourbon and pineapple jam. Serves 2.

Pineapple and Bananas with Cream

3 cups water
1/2 teaspoon vanilla
1 cup sugar
1 (20-ounce) can pineapple chunks
2 bananas, sliced
1 cup heavy cream
2 teaspoons sugar
1 teaspoon dark rum

Bring water, vanilla, and sugar to boil. Lower heat and simmer about 3 minutes. Add pineapple and banana slices and simmer another 2 minutes. Transfer fruit to serving dishes and cool. Reduce syrup by half and pour over fruit. Beat cream until soft peaks form; then add sugar and rum. Continue beating until stiff peaks form. Spoon over fruit. Serves 4.

Gingered Cream over Pineapple

1/2 cup sugar
1/2 cup water
1-1/2-inch piece of fresh ginger, sliced
1 cup whipping cream
1 tablespoon powdered sugar
1/2 teaspoon vanilla
2 cups fresh pineapple chunks

Combine sugar and water in saucepan and heat over medium heat until sugar dissolves. Add ginger slices and simmer another 8 minutes, until syrupy. Remove ginger slices and chill syrup. Whip cream with powdered sugar and vanilla until stiff peaks form. Fold in chilled syrup. Divide pineapple among dessert plates and top with whipped cream mixture. Serves 4.

Molded Pineapple Cheese Cream

12 ounces cream cheese
1 cup heavy whipping cream, whipped
1 (8-ounce) can pineapple rings, drained
Fresh strawberries

Fold together the cheese and the whipped cream. Cut pineapple rings into chunks and fold into cheese. Place in a wet mold and chill overnight. Unmold cheese and garnish with fresh strawberries.

Brandied Pineapple

4 cups fresh pineapple, peeled, cored, and sliced
1 cup sugar
1 cup brandy

Place the pineapple, sugar, and brandy in a sterile glass jar with a closely fitting lid. Store in a cool place not above 45 degrees. Serve over ice cream.

Glazed Pineapple

1 fresh pineapple, peeled, cored, and sliced into rings
1-1/2 cups brown sugar
3 tablespoons honey

Place pineapple rings in saucepan, cover with water and simmer until tender. Reduce liquid to 1 cup and add sugar and honey. Continue simmering until the pineapple is translucent. Drain well; then dry in a 250-degree oven.

Fresh Pineapple in Pineapple Wine

2 cups fresh pineapple cubes
1/4 cup pineapple wine (or other sweet white wine)
Fresh mint sprigs for garnish

Combine pineapple cubes and wine in a glass bowl. Refrigerate at least one hour, stirring occasionally. Serve garnished with the fresh mint. Serves 4.

Pineapple Flambé

4 tablespoons butter
4 tablespoons brown sugar
6 slices fresh pineapple
2 ounces dark rum
Vanilla ice cream

Melt butter, add sugar and cook over low heat for 5 minutes. Add pineapple slices and cook covered until tender. Pour rum over pineapple slices, replace cover and warm the rum for a few moments but do not allow it to boil. Remove cover and ignite by touching edge of pan with a match. Stand back! After flames die down, serve the pineapple over vanilla ice cream. Serves 4.

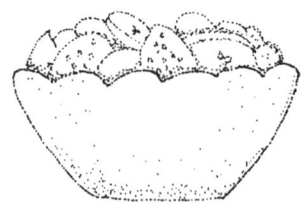

Fruit Fondue

2 cups semisweet chocolate pieces
1 cup evaporated milk
1 teaspoon rum (or vanilla)
1 pineapple, peeled, cored, and cubed
1 pint strawberries
2 bananas, cut into thick slices

In small saucepan heat chocolate, evaporated milk and rum. Keep warm in a fondue pot. Serve surrounded by the fruit pieces to be dunked into the chocolate sauce.

Baked Rhubarb and Pineapple

1 pound diced pink rhubarb
1 (20-ounce) can pineapple chunks, drained and liquid reserved
1/3 cup brown sugar
1/4 cup reserved pineapple liquid
Vanilla ice cream

Combine the first four ingredients in a baking dish. Toss well. Bake at 350 degrees for 25 minutes or until the rhubarb is tender. Serve over vanilla ice cream. Serves 4.

Bread Pudding

2 eggs
1/2 cup sugar
1/4 teaspoon salt
2 cups milk
1 teaspoon vanilla
1 (8-ounce) can crushed pineapple, drained
1/4 cup raisins
2 cups French bread, cubed
2 tablespoons butter
1 cup heavy cream
2 tablespoons sugar
2 teaspoons rum

Combine eggs, sugar, and salt. Add milk and vanilla, mixing well. Toss pineapple, raisins, and bread together. Place bread mixture in buttered baking dish and pour the egg mixture over the top. Stir lightly with a fork to blend. Dot with the butter. Bake at 375 degrees for 25 minutes. While pudding is baking, beat the cream until it thickens. Add the sugar and rum and continue beating until peaks form. Spoon over the warm pudding. Serves 4.

Pineapple Custard Crisps

2 cups whipping cream
2 tablespoons sugar
4 egg yolks
1/2 teaspoon vanilla extract
1/2 teaspoon finely grated orange rind
1 (8-ounce) can pineapple rings
1/4 cup flour
3 tablespoons brown sugar
1/4 teaspoon cinnamon
1/8 teaspoon nutmeg
1/8 teaspoon salt
1/4 cup butter, cut into pieces

Combine cream and sugar in saucepan. Heat, stirring, until sugar dissolves. Simmer for 3 minutes. Beat egg yolks in bowl; gradually whisk in cream mixture. Add vanilla and grated orange rind. Spoon custard into four 1-cup soufflé cups. Place cups in baking pan and add just enough water to come halfway up sides of cups. Bake 30 minutes at 350 degrees. Edges should be set but the centers still shaky. Cover and chill custards. Drain pineapple rings and cut into quarters. Arrange pineapple over custard. Mix flour, brown sugar, cinnamon, nutmeg, salt, and butter until mixture resembles coarse crumbs. Sprinkle topping over the pineapple and custards. Broil about 2 minutes or until golden brown. Chill. Serves 4.

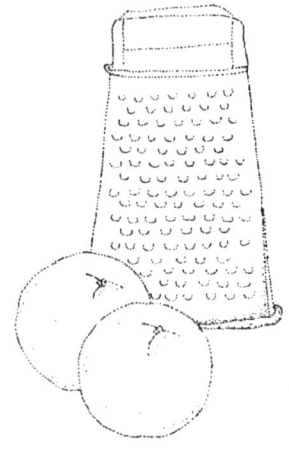

Rice Pudding

1-2/3 cups water
1 cup rice
1 tablespoon butter
1/2 teaspoon salt
2 eggs, beaten
1/3 cup brown sugar
1/2 cup crushed pineapple, drained
Cinnamon

Combine first four ingredients, bring to a boil, reduce heat and simmer. Cook until rice is done. Add beaten eggs, cook 2 minutes, and stir in sugar and pineapple. Pour into dessert cups, sprinkle with cinnamon and chill. Serves 4.

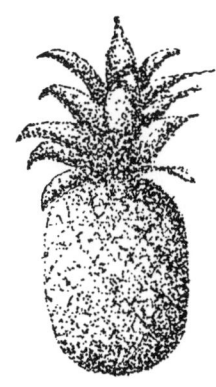

Pineapple Tapioca Pudding

4 tablespoons pearl tapioca
2 cups milk
2 egg yolks
1 (8-ounce) can pineapple tidbits, drained

Combine tapioca, milk, and egg yolks in a saucepan. Bring to a boil, reduce heat and simmer until tapioca is translucent, about 12 minutes. Remove from heat, stir in pineapple, cover and chill. Serves 4.

Pineapple Sorbet

1 pineapple, peeled, cored, and cubed
1/3 cup sugar
1 tablespoon lemon juice
2 tablespoons Grenadine

Purée all of the ingredients in a food processor. Then freeze in an ice cream maker according to manufacturer's directions or freeze in trays until slushy, 1 to 2 hours. Serves 4.

Pineapple-Lime Sorbet

2 cups pineapple juice
Juice and zest of 1 lime
2 kiwifruit, peeled and sliced
4 strawberries, sliced

Combine pineapple juice, lime juice, and zest in an ice cream maker and freeze according to manufacturer's directions or freeze in trays until slushy, 1 to 2 hours. Serve garnished with slices of kiwifruit and strawberries. Serves 4.

Chutney
Jam
Preserves
Relish
and
Salsas

CHUTNEY, JAM, PRESERVES, RELISH, AND SALSA

Pineapple Chutney
Coconut Pineapple Chutney
Spiced Pineapple Chutney
Easy Pineapple Jam
Pineapple Preserves
Melodi's Pineapple Relish
Pineapple Salsa
Pineapple and Papaya Salsa
Pineapple Sauce for Roast Beef
Pineapple Sauce for Ham

Pineapple Chutney

1 (20-ounce) can pineapple chunks, undrained
1 small onion, minced
1/2 teaspoon cinnamon
1/4 teaspoon nutmeg
1/4 teaspoon ginger
1/2 teaspoon cumin
1/2 teaspoon coriander
1/2 teaspoon curry powder
2 tablespoons brown sugar
2 tablespoons lemon juice

Combine pineapple, including liquid from can, and all other ingredients in small saucepan. Bring to a boil, lower heat and simmer uncovered for about 20 minutes. Cool to room temperature and serve.

Coconut Pineapple Chutney

1 cup fresh pineapple, grated
2 tablespoons minced fresh ginger
1 cup minced onions
2/3 cup brown sugar
1/2 cup unsweetened coconut

Combine all ingredients in a food processor or blender and process until smooth.

Spiced Pineapple Chutney

1/2 cup cider vinegar
1/4 cup water
1/4 cup onion, chopped
1 tablespoon fresh ginger, minced
1/2 teaspoon grated orange peel
1 garlic clove, minced
Dash red pepper flakes
3/4 cup brown sugar
1 (20-ounce) can crushed pineapple

Combine first 7 ingredients in a saucepan, bring to a boil, reduce heat and simmer for 10 minutes. Add brown sugar and pineapple; stir until sugar dissolves. Continue cooking until pineapple is soft and the liquid has thickened. Cover and refrigerate. Bring to room temperature before serving.

Easy Pineapple Jam

3/4 cup sugar
3/4 cup water
1 (20-ounce) can crushed pineapple, undrained

In saucepan dissolve sugar in water; add pineapple. Bring to a boil, lower heat and simmer a few minutes. Pour into a jar, cover and refrigerate until ready to use.

Pineapple Preserves

This is a good use for overripe fruit. Just use the best parts and toss out the rest.

1 large fresh pineapple, peeled, cored, and cut into chunks
3 cups sugar
1/2 cup water
2 tablespoons lemon juice

In saucepan stir together the sugar, water, and lemon juice. Add pineapple and cook until the fruit is transparent and the syrup is thick. Stir frequently. Pour into sterile glass jars, cover and store in a cool, dark place.

Melodi's Pineapple Relish

1 (20-ounce) can crushed pineapple
2 cans whole-berry cranberry sauce
1 (16-ounce) package frozen whole strawberries, thawed and drained
1/2 cup chopped walnuts

Mix ingredients in a bowl and chill.

Pineapple Salsa

2 cups fresh pineapple, diced
1/4 cup canned water chestnuts, chopped
3 tablespoons onion, diced
2 teaspoons minced fresh mint
1 teaspoon minced cilantro
1/8 teaspoon chili powder
Dash cayenne
2 tablespoons lime juice
2 teaspoons water

Combine all ingredients, cover and chill.

Pineapple and Papaya Salsa

1 cup fresh pineapple, diced
1 large jalapeño pepper, minced
1 large papaya, diced
1 tablespoon cilantro
1 tablespoon lime juice

Mix all ingredients together; season with salt. Chill well.

Pineapple Sauce for Roast Beef

1 tablespoon butter
1 tablespoon flour
1/4 cup white wine
1/4 cup pineapple juice
1 cup beef broth

Melt butter in saucepan, stir in flour and cook 2-3 minutes. Whisk in remaining ingredients, bring to a boil and cook until thickened. Serve warm.

Pineapple Sauce for Ham

For ham steaks or whole, fully cooked ham. Spoon on 20 minutes prior to end of cooking.

1 (20-ounce) can crushed pineapple in syrup
1/2 cup brown sugar
1/4 cup prepared mustard
2 tablespoons lemon juice
1 tablespoon cornstarch
2 tablespoons water

In saucepan combine pineapple with syrup, brown sugar, mustard, and lemon juice. Dissolve cornstarch in water and add to pineapple mixture. Cook, stirring constantly until thickened. Spoon over ham during last 20 minutes of cooking time.